M000289886

Think! Eat! Act!
A Sea Shepherd Chef's Vegan Recipes

Raffaella Tolicetti

First Printing, July 1, 2014
ISBN: 9781621066668
This is Microcosm #151

Cover and interior design by Meggyn Pomerleau
Edited by Lauren Hage and Joe Biel

All content © Raffaella Tolicetti, 2014
This edition is © by Microcosm Publishing, 2014
Photos by Giacomo Giorgi, Kylie Maguire, Raffa, Georgia Laughton@SDA

Microcosm Publishing
2752 N Williams Ave
Portland, OR 97227

In the Vegan Cookbook series

For a catalog, write or visit
MicrocosmPublishing.com

Distributed in the United States and Canada by Independent Publishers Group
and in Europe by Turnaround.

This book was printed on post-consumer paper by union workers in the United States.

THINK! EAT! ACT!

A SEA SHEPHERD CHEF'S VEGAN RECIPES

Raffaella Tolicetti

TABLE OF CONTENTS

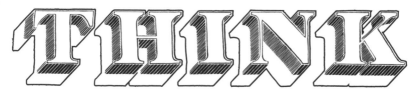

INTRODUCTION 8
COOKED AND RAMMED 10
VEGAN FACTS 13
ANIMALS OF THE SEA 14
ANIMALS ON LAND 16
ENVIRONMENTAL EFFECTS OF ANIMAL AGRICULTURE 18
GARDENING RESISTANCE 20
COOKING FACTS 22

FIRST COURSE 35
PASTA 45
MAIN DISHES 69
SOUPS 109
BREADS 117
DESSERTS 127
RANDOM 138

SEA SHEPHERD CONSERVATION SOCIETY 150
INTERVIEW WITH TOMMY KNOWLES 155
INTERVIEW WITH MARLEY DAVIDUK 158
INTERVIEW WITH JORDAN CROOKE 163
THE HUNT SABOTEURS ASSOCIATION 167
SUPPORT VEGAN PRISONERS 170

INDEX 182
ACKNOWLEDGEMENTS 190

TH1NK

PART 1

INTRODUCTION

I became a cook a bit by chance. I used to cook for myself and my friends after moving away from home when I turned eighteen. I liked it but was never really passionate about it. Then I finished my university degree and decided to join one of Sea Shepherd's ships, which at the time was sailing in the Mediterranean after a blue-fin tuna defense campaign. I was helping on deck but two days after I arrived, the person in charge of the cooking told me that she actually hated cooking, and asked if I could take her spot. I developed a passion for cooking because it became a way for me to express my philosophy about ethics and animals to a lot of people and show them that you can have a beautiful and wide range of food exactly as with any other traditional diet. I also discovered how creative I could be with my hands, and after six years of studying books and theories it felt great to be able to put out something of my own that wouldn't be hand written on a piece of paper.

Back when I was 19, I became vegetarian because I couldn't bear the idea of an animal dying so I could eat it—it just didn't feel right. Since I was a kid I remember fighting against the force-feeding of meat and fish, especially when I could recognize the dead body on my plate. It disgusted me. It took me a few more years to understand the slavery behind animal exploitation, not only for their meat or their skin, but also for their milk, or for their bodies to be tested on. Everything became clear to me when I understood that it is not so much a question of whether our behavior and our habits are legal or not, but whether they are moral or not, and I do not believe that anyone can justify the slaughter and sufferance of billions of animals more easily than injustice in matters of gender equality or human rights.

There are many ways of refusing oppression and cooking is one, because choosing your food is definitely a "political" act. Choosing not to eat animals, not to be part of a system that exploits them, growing your food, or eating organic and local food are many small decisions that make a lot of difference for those who are killed as a consequence of our behavior.

The intent of this book is to make the connection between the food we eat and the ethics that we want to defend. The recipes are complementary to the other parts and couldn't exist without a reflexion on veganism or on activism. Cooking is fun and should definitely be thought of as a pleasure activity, but the simple decision of what to cook is strictly linked to a conscious choice that cannot be ignored.

Many times I have had discussions with my friends or family that in theory agree with most of my beliefs but think it is too difficult to be vegan, or do not fully understand. This book is an attempt to explain the reasons for being vegan, how to be vegan, and what is behind—not only the food, but the activism.

I hope it can help some people open their eyes, as much as it helped me in the past to read books and learn about the cruelty behind the curtains, the one that we don't want to see because it is too painful to admit it even exists.

I believe that if everyone tries their best, things can change and improve, so this is my little contribution!

COOKED AND RAMMED

Cooking on a boat is challenging. Cooking while sailing in Antarctica's rough weather is even more challenging. Cooking while being rammed by a ship eight times as big as yours, in the coldest seas of the planet, brings the challenge to a whole new level. But if all of this is possible, it means that there is nothing as simple as cooking a vegan meal at home.

During the anti-whaling campaign Operation Zero Tolerance, the plan was for our ships to obstruct the illegal refueling of the whaling fleet with their contracted tanker. That way, cutting the source of their energy, we could force them to go back home early in the season, killing as few whales as possible.

But the whaling fleet wasn't going to let us do that, and as tension grew, their factory ship, the Nisshin Maru, collided with us several times in an apparent effort to demolish us so they could go on with their illegal operation.

Every time we got hit it was coincidentally an hour or so before serving a meal, which is the rush time in the galley, so both times we got rammed. I was cooking. The dead lights shut down and there was no possibility of seeing what was happening; the only clues were coming from the bangs that I could hear from outside. As a further coincidence, both collisions happened on the portside stern and on midship, right where the galley is located.

Being rammed by another ship is a scary thought, as you can never be too sure what the damages are going to be until the collision is over, and you do not have a big picture of what is happening. You are just focused on trying to be safe and to make sure that no water is coming in. After taking a few seconds to realize what was actually happening, I turned off all of the electrical equipment, checking that everything was tied down really well, and then went upstairs to sea level. Despite the confusion, it's a moment where everyone and every gesture has to be extremely clear and efficient—you don't want to lose precious seconds in obstructing the deckies and the engineers that are making sure that the boat is still afloat.

Going outside to check the damages, the paradox of the situation hit me vividly. Actions tend to happen on the most beautiful days, when the whaling fleet could get the chance to refuel; an operation possible only in calm seas. All around us is a landscape that inspires serenity and calm, and yet I am as far away as possible from being serene. In between growlers and icebergs, under the striking sun that is almost warm when the wind stops blowing, I can see the monstrous steel floating machine that hit us. In my mind, the ship is a living creature, roaring and steaming with uncontrollable rage and anger; and every time I think of it afterwards, I recall a deadly figure coming out of the ugliest nightmare. I cannot distinguish clearly between the men on board and the ship itself, as they all form one body, surreal, meant to destroy by any means.

And yet we still cook; food is as important as the rest of the efforts during the action, as it brings warmth, energy, and strength. No need to eat animal products to feel strong. The food we cook is vegan because it is a statement that we do not need to make other beings suffer to accomplish our desires, as much as we do not need to destroy the environment to make our way through life.

Neither the whalers nor us are people living in an isolated self-sufficient society relying on animals for their own survival. We can live without cruelty that is unnecessary; we have evolved as a species to a point where we cannot talk about eating animals as part of our survival. We eat animals to satisfy our desires and because we can dominate them easily with our modern technology, affirming our supremacy and our will to reign over everyone and everything. This is true from human to human too; but we have slowly built laws to forbid slavery, gender and ethnic discrimination, or violence against each other. It still happens and probably always will, but the fact that we have created institutions to protect us from each other is a sign of our internal battle, to elevate ourselves to a higher morale where our murder instincts are tempered by reason. Why shouldn't we apply that same logic where animals are concerned? Cruelty is the act of making another being suffer for no rational reason (self defense, survival instinct, etc). Within that definition, animals suffer as much as humans; and the meat, fishing, and dairy industries are responsible for the biggest slaughters that have ever happened on Earth.

It doesn't matter whether we are more intelligent than pigs and cows and tigers and ants (which we are not if you measure intelligence by the relationship you have to your ecosystem). Basing compassion on intelligence is opening the door to the most dangerous theories. What about a kid, with an IQ lower than an adult? What about an adult itself with a low IQ? Do they deserve to die from our hands because they look inferior to our eyes and thus less valuable?

We are the only species that have taken the law of the strongest as the law of the meanest. Animals kill each other in the wild because they need to eat; animals do not slaughter and eradicate another species for the sake of doing it and how it feels to do it. Animals still hunt the same ways they were thousands of years ago; they haven't invented weapons of mass destruction that can not only kill them all, but also kill us all. We invented the animal "industry." Scientific research is based on massive killing, domestication, and slavery on a scale that kills billions each year. We overkill, waste, destroy, all in the name of human progress....

Well, the real progress is to acknowledge our evolution and recognize that we can, and we should, live on vegetarian and vegan diets and survive... and even more, feel better!

VEGAN FACTS

Being vegan means refusing to see animals merely as a product for us to use, and not supporting animal cruelty

(as much as refusing human cruelty—we are animals too).
It means not consuming animal by-products for food as well as for clothing, cosmetic, medicine, and other consumption.

There are different viewpoints on what's vegan, and every individual should make a decision with their own conscience about what is the right behavior to have towards the Earth, animals, and other beings. The point of vegan outreach is not to impose anything, but to give an alternate view and emphasize the importance and impact of our daily choices. It's not about being the perfect vegan; it's about using our brain in an independent way to make actions that are not harmful towards animals, humans, and the earth.

It is important to underline that I am talking as a "westerner"— someone who can get access to an infinite range of choices, without having to worry about whether I'll have food on my plate tomorrow. I am aware of my luck and that this book can only reach certain people, but I do believe that a conscious choice of diet, like veganism, where food is distributed more properly, is one of the solutions to world hunger. There are more than 850 million people that are under-nourished in the world but a lot of food is wasted, and entire fields are purposed for only feeding animals—the same animals that are destined to feed westerners. Due to the industrialization of intensive farming, there is a growing need for space in farmland, causing the expropriation and displacement of millions of people. The use of heavy pesticides and chemical products in modern agriculture causes soil erosion and desertification in many areas, which are now infertile and polluted.

On the next page is a list of facts to illustrate how much cruelty animal consumption induces and how by stop eating animals we could start to re-distribute food equally.

The vocabulary used is taken from official data and reflects the idea that animals are only tools for use and abuse as much as any other "thing" without a soul. I have kept it to show the materialism that is behind most of the studies, which do not aim to respect animals but are worried about how humankind will face the lack of resources if we continue on this path of exponential growth. Thinking of fish as "stock" or cows as "cattle," shows no consideration for life as an individuality but merely as a mass production commodity.

Thanks to my friend Susan for helping me put the facts together.

-ANIMALS OF THE SEA-

The exploitation of the oceans and the animals of the sea can be seen with two different perspectives, which can be illustrated through different facts.

The first perspective is that animals of the sea are divided in people's mind. Mammals are mostly considered sentient beings while the other sea creatures are seen as ours to be consumed and exploited.

Fish are often considered "non-animals" and sometimes offered as a vegetarian option. The fact that fishes are counted in tons and not as individuals is a clear indication of how little they are considered a sentient being that can feel pain and suffer.

The second perspective is the more global approach to the ocean's exploitation and destruction, which includes large-scale fisheries, poaching, over fishing, but also pollution, over traffic, and destruction of the habitat, which altogether leads to a serious threat of extinction and desertification of the sea.

- About 100 million sharks are killed each year. That's approximately 275,000 per day, the equivalent of the entire population of a medium city, with 1 out of 15 sharks getting killed by fisheries.

- It is estimated that at least 90 to 100 million tons of fishes are killed every year. The Food and Agriculture Organization estimates the annual catch for 2011 to be 154 millions tons (both from capture and aquaculture), of which 131 are destined for human consumption.

- In the past 50 years we have eaten more than 90% of the big fishes. The world fish food supply has grown dramatically in the last five decades, with an average growth rate of 3.2 percent per year from 1961–2009, outpacing the increase of 1.7 percent per year in the world's population.

- 60 to 75% of the world's fisheries are fully or over-exploited

- Sonar in the oceans is the cause of death to many cetaceans, provoking damages to the tissues, to the livers and kidneys which leads to decompression sickness which is fatal to many sea animals

- 80% of the coral reef has disappeared due to overfishing and land-derived pollution since the beginning of the 20th century

- Bluefin tuna, a top predator of the sea, have been reduced by more than 82 percent. The International Commission for the Conservation of Atlantic Tunas (ICCAT) estimates that as few as 25,000 individual mature Bluefin tuna remain, although the proposal to ban its international trade as an endangered species has been rejected. Among the seven principal tuna species, one-third are estimated to be over-exploited.

- The disappearance of the predators of the sea leads to a threat to the ecosystem with the uncontrollable growth of algae, jellyfish, or smaller fishes, causing an "ecological imbalance."

- Six species of turtles are listed as endangered under the Endangered Species Act. Each year, more than 250,000 endangered Loggerhead and Leatherback turtles are caught by long-lines worldwide.

- Krill (both as an oil and as a meal) is food for many animals and therefore harvested for fish farming. It is also used by human consumption for its oil. It is hard to find global data, as commercial operations only exist for Antarctic krill, caught in one of the most pristine and fragile environment of the world. In 2007, 118,124 tons were caught around Antarctica.

- About 25% of fish caught are considered "by-catch" and thrown back dead into the sea, mainly because driftnets, which are up to 50 km long, catch anything from small species to big cetaceans like dolphins, and are extremely devastating for marine wildlife as a result. Driftnets are banned on high seas and their size is limited on other seas but the lack of ability to police their use globally allows fisherman to still use them heavily around the globe.

- Farmed fish, or aquaculture, consume 53% of the fish population. It takes about three kg of fish to feed one kg of farmed salmon, and the ratio rises to twenty to one for tuna. Out of 200, eight of the farmed species use 62% of the total fish food.

- Farmed fish are food for many land-farmed animals, as "animal feed." But farmed fishes also rely on terrestrial animal protein meals and oils, leading to a situation where we farm land animals for aquaculture and farm water animals for factory farming.

- In the last three decades aquaculture has expanded by almost 264%. About 600 species are raised in captivity in 190 different countries for production in the farming system

- Long-line is another cruel and wasteful fishing method. It is made of a line with baited hooks all the way down, and it stays in the sea until the fishermen come back later to retrieve its victims. Used mainly for catching medium fishes, the long-lines kill seabirds, turtles, and sharks by the thousands.

-ANIMALS ON LAND-
Number of Animals Killed

- Worldwide: (by weight) 2011: 297 million tons

- United States: (by head count): 2012/approximately 9 billion
    *this number does not include rabbits or horses, as the United States Department of Agriculture (the body that regulates animal agriculture in the U.S.) does not keep track of those numbers.

Meat Consumption

- Worldwide: (on average) 42.3 kilos (93.3 pounds)
- United States: 200 pounds each year per person, roughly half-pound per day, 52 billion pounds total

Meat Production

- 2010 - 294.2 million tons
- 2011 - 297.1 million tons

Milk Production

- 2010 - 722.9 million tons
- 2011 - 733.9 million tons

Factory Farming (AKA CAFO—Concentrated Animal Feeding Operations; "Factory Farm" is used by animal rights advocates and environmentalists, CAFO is the industry term for intensive confinement).

- The United States Environmental Protection Agency defines farms as Animal Feeding Operations (AFO) when they "confine animals for at least 45 days in a 12-month period, and have no grass or other vegetation in the confinement area." They are considered a CAFO when they "are over a certain size, have a stream running through the facility, or discharge waste into water in the United States."

- According to the United States Environmental Protection Agency, CAFOs in the United States generate 500 million tons of manure each year. This is three times the amount of waste that the EPA estimates is generated by humans annually in the same country.

- According to the EPA, there are 15,500 CAFOs in the United States. The number of CAFOs is on the rise worldwide. They are now the fastest growing system for farm animal production. 72% of poultry production, 43% of egg production, and 55% of pork production occurs on CAFOs.

ENVIRONMENTAL EFFECTS OF ANIMAL AGRICULTURE

- Animal agriculture is responsible for 18% of the world's greenhouse gas emissions. This includes 9% of the carbon dioxide created, as well as 40% of methane and 65% of nitrous oxide production. Methane has a warming potential 25 times higher than carbon dioxide; nitrous oxide has a warming potential 300 times more potent than carbon dioxide.[11]

- Cattle production has been the cause of 65-80% of the deforestation of the Amazon.[11]

- Livestock production utilizes 8% of global human water usage.

- The livestock industry is the largest source of water pollution, namely animal wastes, antibiotics, hormones, chemicals from tanneries, fertilizers, pesticides from food crops, and sediments from eroded pastures.[12]

Health Effects of Animal Agriculture/ Benefits of a Plant Based Diet

- In the United States, 29 million pounds of antibiotics are fed to livestock each year. This is estimated to be around 80% of the U.S.'s total antibiotic use. This overuse of antibiotics has been linked to increased amounts of antibiotic resistant bacteria.

- Vegetarian diets offer a number of nutritional benefits including lower levels of saturated fat, cholesterol, and animal protein as well as higher levels of carbohydrates, fiber, magnesium, potassium, folate, antioxidants such as vitamins C and E, and phytochemicals. Vegetarians have been reported to have lower body mass indexes than non-vegetarians, as well as lower rates of death from ischemic heart disease, lower blood cholesterol levels, lower blood pressure, and lower rates of hypertension, type 2 diabetes, prostate and colon cancer.

Many vegan foods contain ingredients that are damaging to the environment and to animals. Palm oil is a good example of those aliments that can be deleterious and it is interesting to keep in mind that as a few aspects of it make it not vegan-friendly.

The palm oil issue in numbers:
- Palm oil was discovered in 1848
- The 1980s saw the beginning of massive plantations of it in Borneo and Sumatra
- Malaysia and Indonesia produce 85% of the world's palm oil and are two of the world's biggest carbon dioxide emitters as a result.
- 50 million tons of palm oil is produced every year
- The average western citizen consumes about 10 kg of palm oil each year; palm oil is hidden under a lot of different names
- Roundtable on Sustainable Palm Oil (RSPO) lists in its stakeholders companies like Unilever, McDonald's, Proctor & Gamble, Johnson & Sons, Colgate-Palmolive.
- 5,000 Bornean Orangutans and 1,000 Sumatran Orangutans are killed each year due to palm oil plantation
- An area the size of 300 football fields of rainforest is cleared each hour in Indonesia and Malaysia for palm oil plantation
- 90% of the orangutans habitat was destroyed in the last 20 years, and is projected to be gone within the next 20 years

Like GMO soybeans grown to feed the animals that are meant to be slaughtered, or any other massive plantations that will destroy the entire ecosystem of an area, it is good to think before buying products that contain palm oil. Most westerners live a life which is, in many aspects, not vegan friendly: commuting by car, travelling by plane, being addicted to new technologies that verge on the "consume-and-throw-away-every-six-months" dynamic, buying GMO products, eating packaged foods, going to the supermarket, and buying unseasonable goods. It's enough to cause obsession about these behaviors and their cruel side-effects. It is important to always question our habits and make careful decisions to know the results of our consumption.

For me, being vegan is a path; something I can always improve because the more I grow up, the more I understand issues that I had no idea about before. The solution lies not only in being vegan, but also in consuming less—that's a complementary key to a vegan diet. Veganism can only make sense within a global effort to change our way of living drastically.

GARDENING RESISTANCE

A year or so ago I started to visit Annie at her small but flourishing backyard garden in the suburbs of Melbourne, so she could teach me the basics of gardening. I needed to know more about the steps that come before the cooking, the growing of the vegetables and herbs, a whole world forgotten in the era of the supermarket.

I grew up first in Paris, then in Rome, and although I was lucky enough to have grandparents who lived in the countryside and to get a little taste of nature every holiday, my knowledge of basic things such as plants and flowers was very limited.

I felt the growing curiosity to learn what was behind the curtain, to understand where everything I was cooking and eating came from, in a desire to have a stronger connection with something I felt was buried deep inside of me, like a survival instinct that had not totally been destroyed by years of concrete and city.

There was also the awakening of my conscience, who couldn't pretend to be doing something better for the environment, for the animals and in general for the Earth if I didn't start to shake my urban behavior into something more honest that made me open my eyes to the reality of the food system.

After the second World War, agriculture was turned into an industrialized system of mass production and some multinationals started to get more and more power, invading the market with pesticides, herbicides, and genetically modified organisms. This had an extremely negative impact on small farmers, consumers, animals, and the environment. The first are enslaved to GMO seeds and forced to rely on monoculture or to quit; the latter end up eating things that cannot even be called food anymore; as for the animals and the environment, they get even less consideration and we are assisting in the over-exploitation of our ecosystem, due to massive pollution, contamination, and its destruction.

Marie Mason is an environmental activist serving nearly 22 years prison sentence for the destruction of equipment related to Monsanto-funded research on GMOs. No one was hurt or injured during this action and the sentence is trying to send a clear message from the big multinationals that feel their business is being threatened by people from all around the world who refuse to submit to this alienation.

Growing your own vegetables is a way to stand against this enslavement of the food and agriculture system, as well as a pleasant way of re-connecting with nature. Not everyone has the chance to have their own little backyard but more and more cities are doing shared or community gardens, giving everyone a little patch to plant on.

Grow your veggies!!

Here are Annie's seven tips about starting your own garden or patch:

1. Start small
2. Pamper the soil
3. Plant leafy greens to start
4. Grow "cut and come again" for continuous harvest
5. Aim to grow from organic seeds
6. Compost or have a worm farm
7. Encourage bees and pollination by planting flowers

You can go online to learn more
about organic gardening,
check in your local community!

COOKING FACTS

Be creative. Every recipe is inspired by another, and every new recipe will inspire another one. In this book you might find different inspirations; I tried to include invented recipes as much as possible, but there is no such thing as a totally new recipe, as any idea is influenced by what I've seen, tasted, and learned before. And this is fine, because the point is to share ideas to make the world tastier!

I am an olive oil nut, everyone I've cooked with can say that. Not that I am proud of it, but extra virgin olive oil is the only ingredient I cannot cook without. No margarine, no sauces, no nothing, I don't care.... as long as I have some good olive oil. An Italian chef once said, "If something goes wrong, just add some olive oil." I couldn't agree more. Olive oil makes your life better, and you can use it for your skin too, so olive oil it is. I also like coconut oil. Stay away as much as possible from palm oil and all the shitty oils. They're bad for you and for the environment.

This sounds silly, but use your hands; you have to feel the food that you are making. Touching is as important as tasting, so as long as your hands are clean, go and feel!

I try to have a healthy, balanced diet, mainly because I like it and this is how I have always eaten. I try to avoid white sugar, processed, and deep-fried food. This does not take much effort, as I prefer natural sugar from fruit, raw, or slightly cooked meals, whole grain flour rather than white, and I am not a big fan of fake meat or fake cheese. However, cooking on a ship for a lot of different people, I've had to learn to make a lot of different food that I would never have made before—in fact, I had no idea it existed. This is especially true for desserts—I'd still rather make and eat kilos of pasta than cupcakes. But as said before, you can change a recipe, put less sugar, or substitute with applesauce and healthy stuff. Although once in a while you might as well go for a naughty treat—eating is not about punishing ourselves, so I'd rather have too many calories and a long bike ride right after than forbid myself some of the pleasures of life!

Simple is good. Do not overdo anything. My favorite cooking is Italian, and this is because daily Italian cooking is simple. You can still taste the ingredients, they are not drowning in sauces and herbs and oil that kill the flavors (although sometimes there is an excess of oil!). If I cooked just for myself I would only make simple dishes, like spinach with lemon, pasta with fresh tomatoes and garlic, salads, and so on. If you can rely on local and organic ingredients instead of plastic tomatoes from the supermarket, there is no need to overcook, the first step of cooking is already done just by choosing your ingredients.

I haven't put any salad recipes in this book, not that I don't like salads, but I feel it is the easiest dish to be creative with. It's nice to mix colors, add nuts and seeds and sprouts, and to come out with a unique dish, so I never really think about what I put in a salad, and it's never the same twice. Although I particularly love spinach salad with mushrooms, fresh basil, lemon juice, nutritional yeast, a little olive oil (I warned you!), and soy sauce.

Do it yourself as much as possible—that way you reduce packaging and artificial ingredients and a lot of other nasty things for the environment.

Having a soy or rice milk maker is a good investment for the long term if you use a lot of non-dairy milk. Same with a good blender, homemade smoothies are one thousand times better than plastic bottled ones. I am astonished by the quantity of garbage we throw away every day, and how little is recyclable. So, with little steps, we can all improve our daily consumption, starting by consuming less and avoiding certain products. Go to the source and make your food from scratch. It will taste better, be healthier, and be more satisfying. Most of us were born in the years of the supermarket culture, where every thing is plackaged in plastic and you need a degree in chemistry to read the ingredients list. For some products there are more numbers than natural ingredients—and you need a guide to determine if they are vegan or not. By buying as much as possible directly at the farmers market, you can avoid eating "plastic food."

We tend to believe that we are not able to cook or that a recipe is too complicated and needs so many ingredients that we don't have. It's not true. You can make almost everything at home with basic ingredients.

For years I have been cooking on ships that rely on cooking what was donated to us, not what I chose to buy. Using wholefood ingredients you can make as much good food as what is offered by big companies. It is just a matter of understanding a few tricks and playing in the kitchen!

A few recipes are underlined as raw. I eat quite a lot of raw food because I have days where I feel that I need to detox my body. This is because cooking can remove approximately 30% of your food's nutrients and all the enzymes present in the food. They break with the heat. A diet that includes raw food is rich in alkalising foods, like greens, fruits, and sprouts that are good for cleansing and detoxification.

Making your own sprouts is a good way access cheap and easy raw food. Lentils and chickpeas are easy to sprout—soak them overnight, place in a jar or bucket with a net on top, and rinse two to three times per day for three to four days.

WHERE TO ACCESS ESSENTIAL NUTRIENTS IN A VEGAN DIET

CALCIUM

helps: skeleton constitution (bones and teeth), muscle development, neurotransmitter release

Sources: cabbage!! (around 60% of daily needs), almonds, soy and soy derivates, green beans, hemp seeds, seaweed (wakame, kombu, kelp), molasses, dried figs, chickpeas, sunflower seeds, hazelnut, pistachios, rutabaga, okra, broccoli, sesame

MAGNESIUM

helps: bone fortification, enzyme production, DNA synthesis

sources: greens (chlorophyll), bread, quinoa, nutritional yeast, nuts, dark chocolate, bran, oats, buckwheat

OMEGA 3 AND 6

helps: prevention of heart diseases, asthma, muscular degeneration

sources: seeds (flax, chia, hemp), nuts (pecan, walnut, hazelnut, cashew, pine nut), corn, soybeans, vegetable oil (especially linseed oil), hemp oil, broccoli, cabbage, black raspberry, kiwi fruit, butternut, avocados, cereal, durum wheat, acai berry, spirulina, coconut

ATTENTION: Flaxseed=linseed

PROTEIN

helps: catalysing metabolic reactions, DNA replication, stimulus response, transporting molecules from one location to another, source of amino acids

sources: dry beans, quinoa, soy products (tofu, miso, TVP), cereals, nuts, gluten

IRON

helps: haemoglobin production, to carry oxygen from lungs to tissues

sources: tofu, bean sprouts, nuts, dark leafy greens, molasses, quinoa, dry fruit, lentils, pistachios

ATTENTION: Spinach and swiss chard contain iron but they also contain oxalates, that makes iron almost unavailable for absorption.

SODIUM

helps: (maintain stable) blood pressure, balance of water in the body, nerves and muscle contraction.

Avoid food that is too salty!
Sources: vegetables, fruits, nuts

PHOSPHORUS

helps: needed in conjunction with Vitamin C in order for Vitamin C to be utilized by the body.

sources: greens, bread, nutritional yeast, nuts, quinoa, soy

ZINC

helps: protein synthesis, hormones, skin, immune system

sources: wheat germ, nutritional yeast, cashew, brazil nuts, hemp seed, pumpkin seed, sunflower seed, quinoa, dry beans

VITAMIN D

helps: regulation of calcium and phosphorus, heart function, blood coagulation

source: sun (15 min a day), you can find it in fortified products like: margarine, veg milks, cereals

VITAMIN B2 (or riboflavin)

helps: energy metabolism, skin, lips, and eyes

sources: rice, wholemeal flours, mushrooms, nutritional yeast, leaf vegetables, asparagus, popcorn, bananas, persimmons, okra, chard, legumes, tomatoes, almonds

VITAMIN B12

helps: cell division, DNA synthesis, myelin formation, brain and nervous system

ATTENTION: Neither fungi, plants, or animals are capable of the production of B12, only bacteria and archea have the enzymes required for its synthesis, so they are its only form in nature. Its assimilation occurs thanks to a protein produced by the stomach. Deficiencies can occur in omnivores, vegetarians, and/or vegans for various reasons. Problems that can occur as a result of deficiencies are aenemia and problems with nervous system function.

sources: nutritional yeast, miso, spirulina, sprouts—are not an active and reliable source. B12 is better found in supplements and fortified foods.

VITAMIN B1 (or thiamine)

helps: energy, nervous system

sources: brown rice, whole meal flours, nuts and seeds, nutritional yeast, asparagus, kale, cauliflower, potatoes, oranges, oatmeal, flaxseed, sunflower seeds

ATTENTION: Is lost easily, for example when rice is cooked, the B1 is leached into the cooking water. It is also lost if the food is mixed with bicarbonate soda. Tea and coffee are anti-thiamine foods!!

VITAMIN A

helps: skin and cellular health, immune function, vision, gene transcription, antioxidant, embryonic development and reproduction, bone metabolism

sources: carrot, pumpkin, sweet potatoes, spinach, mango, capsicum, margarine (not cooked), dandelion greens, kale, collard greens, cantaloupe, apricot, papaya, pea, tomatoes

VITAMIN E

helps: is an antioxidant

sources: nuts, seeds, soy, olive oil, vegetable oil, spinach, turnip, beet, collard, dandelion greens, avocados, grapefruit, pumpkin, sweet potatoes, mangos, tomatoes

VITAMIN B6

helps: protein conversion, production of haemoglobin in the blood

sources: dry beans, whole grains, nuts, raisins, bananas, nutritional yeast

ATTENTION: Cooked and processed food loses up to 50% of B6

POTASSIUM

helps: heart function, blood pressure, maintains fluid and electrolyte balance in the body

sources: banana, whole grain, raisins, muesli, root plant, lentils, kiwi fruit, orange, potato, coconut, avocado, apricots, parsnip, turnip

FOLATE (or vitamin B9 or vitamin m)

helps: blood, cell division and growth, prevents birth defects and DNA synthesis

sources: chickpeas, nuts, almonds, hazelnuts, oranges, bananas, broccoli, nutritional yeast, spinach, turnips, leaf vegetables, lettuce, sunflower seeds, bok choy, brussel sprouts

VITAMIN B3 (or niacin)

helps: energy production, skin, nervous system

sources: wholemeal flours, peas, sesame seeds, nutritional yeast, avocados, dates, broccoli, carrots, tomatoes, sweet potatoes, asparagus, leaf vegetables, shitake mushrooms, yeast extract, peanut butter, nuts, tofu, soy sauce

VITAMIN C

helps: collagen synthesis (skin, bones, teeth), immune function, wound healing, antioxidant—which protect us from free radicals (cancer prevention)

sources: lemon, oranges, grapefruit, kiwi, passion fruit, lettuce, parsley, tomato, cabbage, cauliflower, broccoli, spinach, papaya, strawberry, garlic, melon, kale, mandarins, lime, mango, grapefruit, raspberry, potato, cranberry, blueberry, pineapple

VITAMIN K

helps: blood coagulation, bones, tissues

sources: greens like kale, dandelions, spinach, collard, broccoli, endive, romaine lettuce, asparagus, mustard greens, cabbage, spinach, oil, margarine

For more information:
http://pcrm.org/health/diets/vegdiets/vegetarian-foods-powerful-for-health

EAT

PART 2

FIRST

36	SPICY BROCCOLI CREAM
37	BORLOTTI BALSAMIC CREAM
38	EGGPLANT CAVIAR
40	SPRING ROLLS
43	ZUCCHINI CARPACCIO

PASTA

47	PENNE TOMATO BASIL EGGPLANT AND VEG RICOTTA
48	SPAGHETTI ALLA CARBONARA
50	PESTO SPAGHETTI/LASAGNA
52	RIGATONI WITH RED BELL PEPPER CREAM
53	TOMATO CREAMY LO'S PASTA
54	CURRIED ZUCCHINI CARROTS PASTA
56	RED PESTO PASTA
59	RAVIOLI SPINACH RICOTTA AND WALNUTS
61	PASTA BROCCOLI POTATOES AND WALNUTS
62	ASPARAGUS CREAM LASAGNA
65	TOMATO LASAGNA WITH CHICKPEA RAGU
66	SPAGHETTI GARLIC CHILI AND OIL

MAIN DISHES

71	GARDEN RISOTTO
72	VEGGIE GATEAU
74	POTATO CROQUETTES
76	ONION PIE
78	QUINOA POTATO AND SHITAKE
81	GLUTEN FREE BURGERS
82	POTATO PATTIES
85	POTATOES AND CARROTS PUREE WITH CARMELIZED ONIONS
86	SAMOSAS
88	CANNELLINI AL FIASCO
90	PUMPKIN GNOCCHI
92	MOMOKO'S JAPANESE CURRY
94	SAVORY FILLLED CREPES
96	VEGGIE FRITTI
97	ROASTED POTATOES, MUSHROOMS, AND GREEN BEANS IN WHITE WINE
98	PARMIGIANA
100	MINI FOREST PIES
102	POTATO TARO CAULIFLOWER COCONUT GRATIN
103	POTATO SALAD WITH PAPRIKA TOFU MAYO
104	SEITAN IN RED WINE SAUCE
106	SEITAN SCHNITZELS
107	FREE THE BOEUF BOURGUIGNON STEW
108	SPINACH QUICHE

SOUP

MASSAMAN TOFU MUSHROOM SOUP	111
SPINACH GAZPACHO	112
SALMOREJO	113
CARROT SOUP	113
MISO SOUP	114

BREAD

BRUSCHETTE	118
FOCACCIA/PIZZA	120
GARLIC SCROLLS	122
PIZZA CRACKERS	124
SPINACH BRAID BREAD	125

DESSERT

CORDOBES ORANGE DESSERT	127
OAT MACADAMIA CHOCOLATE COOKIES	128
DATE AND ALMOND BALLS	129
RAISINS SNAILY SNAP	131
TIRAMISU	132
NO BAKE CHOCO-PEANUT PIE	133
CROSTATA	134
CHOCOLATE LOG	137

RANDOM

BECHAMELLE	138
ICED COCCONUCCINO	138
VEG RICOTTA	139
KALE CHIPS	139
CHICKPEA OMELETTE/FARINATA	141
MORNING TOFU	142
MORNING SMOOTHIE	143

I usually use the American measuring system when I cook. Here are a few basic items with conversion, useful if you use a European measurement system:

WEIGHT
Flour (all purpose): 1 CUP = 125 gram
Flour (sifted): 1 CUP = 100gr
Sugar (granulated): 1 CUP = 225 gr
Sugar (raw): 1 CUP = 180 gr
Cocoa powder: 1 CUP = 125 gr

LIQUID
1 tsp (tsp): = 5 ml
1 tablespoon (Tbsp): = 15 ml
Water: 1 CUP = 250 ml

TEMPERATURE
320 to 325 Fahrenheit = 160 Celsius
350 to 355 Fahrenheit = 180 Celsius
395 to 400 Fahrenheit = 200 Celsius

The recipes are mainly for four to six people.

For pie or cake I use an eleven inch round tray = 30 cm
For rectangular cake I use an 11 x 7 x 2 inch tray = 28x7 cm
For savory baking I use a rectangular 13 x 9 x 2 inch tray = 33 x 23 cm
For loaf I use a 9 x 5 x 3 inch tray = 23 x 23 x 8 cm

For the weight, both solid and liquid, I have kept the two measurements, in ounce/liquid ounces and grams/liter, sometimes approximating to make it easier.

FIRST COURSE

Spicy Broccoli Cream

SOY FREE WHEAT FREE

1 broccoli head, chopped
3 cloves of garlic
1 tsp chili
1 cup water
extra virgin olive oil
salt

Heat the oil, chili, and the garlic cloves in a pan over medium heat. Add the broccoli and cook for a minute. Add half a cup of water and cook until the broccoli is tender. Put in a food processor or a blender with the remaining water and blend until smooth. Add salt and serve over bruschetta, sandwich, or as a dip.

BORLOTTI BALSAMIC CREAM

1 ½ cups borlotti beans
water
¼ cup balsamic vinegar
2 Tbsp olive oil
salt
rosemary (optional)

Soak the beans overnight. Rinse them, cover with water, and bring to a boil. Reduce the heat to medium and cook until tender, making sure they don't dry out by adding a little water from time to time.
When cooked, add the balsamic vinegar and the olive oil and blend until creamy and season with salt. Serve warm or cold with a drizzle of olive oil and some rosemary on top.
It makes a good spread for sandwiches.

Eggplant Caviar

SOY FREE

WHEAT FREE

5 small eggplants
1 lemon's juice
2 Tbsp tahini
salt

Preheat the oven to 400° F / 200° C. When it's ready, put the eggplants on a tray and roast them whole for about 30 minutes. When the skin begins to wrinkle, take them out, let them cool, and then peel. Blend the eggplants with the lemon juice and tahini in a food processor. Add salt and serve cold—possibly with more lemon juice on top.

Spring Rolls

SOY FREE · WHEAT FREE · RAW

3 silverbeet leaves
1/2 cucumber
1 purple carrot
1 green pepper
fresh mint
alfalfa sprouts

For the dip:
2 Tbsp sunflower seeds
8 Tbsp water
4 Tbsp of braggs or tamari
1 tsp apple cider vinegar

5,000 years ago carrots were not orange. They were purple, yellow, red, and black and cultivated in the area now known as Afghanistan, not for the root but for the properties of their leaves. They are rich in antioxidants, and have a lot of other health benefits: anti-inflammatory, anti-bacterial, just to say a few but the list goes on. If you can't find any, replace with beetroot.

Remove the stalks from the silverbeet leaves.
Cut each leaf into four pieces, so your three leaves turn into twelve pieces.
Cut the veggies into thin sticks, removing the seeds from the cucumber.
Don't peel the carrots, just rub them under the water, as a lot of the nutrition is found in the skin.
Fill each leaf with the veggies, a little bit of fresh chopped mint, and some alfalfa sprouts. Roll the leaf so it seals.
Blend the sunflower seeds with the water and add the rest of the ingredients. Dip the rolls in the sauce with every bite that you take!

Alfalfa sprouts are easy to make at home! Buy the seeds. Soak them between six to eight hours in a glass jar covered with a cloth. Rinse them twice a day, without soaking them anymore; if you are in a hot environment, rinse them three times so they don't dry out. After four or five days they should be sprouted and ready to eat. Alfalfa sprouts have many nutritional values, as they act as an antioxidant, an anti-inflammatory, an anti-fatigue, a digestive aid, and much more; they contain a lot of vitamin K, essential for blood coagulation, and a lot of minerals, and a high level of chlorophyll. Alfalfa sprouts have a higher nutritional value than lettuce and therefore are precious on a ship where you run out of fresh food after some time!

ZUCCHINI CARPACCIO

> 2 medium zucchinis
> 1 cup sundried tomatoes
> handful of fresh basil
> ½ cup pecans
> 1 fresh tomato
> ¼ red pepper
> 1 garlic clove
> dash of fresh lemon juice
> olive oil

Slice the zucchini really thin, by hand or with a food processor.
Put on a big serving tray.
Blend all the other ingredients into a pesto.
Mix the pesto with the zucchini,
making sure that the pesto is evenly distributed.
Refrigerate at least two hours before serving.

I love pasta in all its forms.
The cooking is a big part in making the pasta delicious.
I hate to eat overcooked pasta no matter how good the sauce is.
So here are a few tips:

- Measure roughly half a liter of water per 100 grams of pasta. This is to make sure there is enough water during the cooking so the pasta doesn't stick together. It is very important.

- When the water is boiling, add some coarse salt (I put a half handful per 500 grams of pasta, or 3 Tablespoons). Use a little less if you include some vegetable stock. Wait for the water to boil again, so the salt is dissolved and distributed in the water.

- Don't cook with a lid. Just put the pasta in when your water is boiling after you put the salt in.

- When the pasta is in the water, stir the pasta a few times so it doesn't stick together. Some people add a little oil but if you use enough water and stir the pasta sufficiently it won't stick, even for big quantities.

- DO NOT OVERCOOK! Whole-wheat pasta takes a little longer, usually more than ten minutes, while white flour pasta takes usually less than ten minutes to cook. Try the pasta two minutes before the indicated time. It is better to have an al dente pasta because you can recook it in a pan with the sauce (actually certain recipes call for the second cooking of the pasta in the pan, in which case take it out a minute or so before it's done).

- Drain the pasta in a colander, and if you can, keep the water in the sink to wash the dishes afterwards.

- Do not pour cold water over the pasta. When drained, mix in a bowl with the sauce or cook in a pan on low heat with the sauce for another minute. The sauce has to be served with the pasta, not aside!!

PASTA

PENNE TOMATO BASIL EGGPLANT AND VEG RICOTTA (PASTA ALLA NORMA)

Normal sauce:
3 small eggplants
18 ounces (or 500 grams) small tomatoes (cherry tomato)
5 garlic cloves, minced
2 handfuls fresh basil, half minced half to keep for decorating
2 tsp chili flakes
extra virgin olive oil
Vegan Ricotta (see Ricotta recipe, pg. 139)
35 ounces (or 1 kg) penne

Cut the eggplants lengthwise in slices of about a 1/2" / 1 cm thick. Grill them in a pan with no oil—this makes the pasta healthier than fried eggplants.
Grill on both sides for a few minutes, remove, and cut into small pieces. In a pan, heat some olive oil, garlic, basil, and chili. When the kitchen starts to smell delicious like Italy, add the tomato (whole) and crush with a fork. Cook on medium heat for about two minutes and add the eggplants. Cook a few minutes, add salt, and put aside.
Make the vegan ricotta and add to the sauce.
When the pasta is cooked, add the sauce, a little bit of raw olive oil, and the rest of the basil to decorate as well as a little ground black pepper.
You can add some chili if you like it more spicy.
Buon appetito!

SPAGHETTI ALLA CARBONARA

This is an authentic Italian pasta dish but the original version is far from vegan. It calls for both eggs and meat, and I cannot imagine how heavy it is to eat. I might have had it when I was a kid but I cannot remember at all—I just know that I love this vegan version of it! It took me a while to figure out how to make it. The vegetarian version is with zucchini or seitan; but still eggs. I prefer the zucchini to the seitan as it is way lighter and I can eat tons without feeling that my stomach is drowning into my socks afterwards, but if you have some smoked seitan you can use it instead of the zucchini. The problem of eggs remains. I started with scrambled tofu, but since I have found out that I could scramble the veg ricotta, it was illuminating; the perfect combination. So here it goes:

1 big zucchini
2 red onions
olive oil
Veg Ricotta (see p. 139)
salt
quite a lot of black pepper
dash of Tabasco (optional)
18 ounces (or 500 gr) spaghetti

Put some water to boil for the pasta.
Chop the zucchini in little chunks, not too big. Chop the onions and sauté in a pan with olive oil. When they are frying, add the zucchini and cook until they are slightly brown.
Meanwhile, prepare the ricotta according to the recipe. Scramble it in a separate pan with turmeric, nutritional yeast, oil, black pepper, and a dash of Tabasco.
Add the scrambled ricotta to the onion and zucchini sauce and mix for a few minutes on low heat. Add salt and pepper.
When the pasta is cooked, strain, and mix all together and add a little more black pepper and if necessary a little bit of olive oil.
Serve straight away.

PESTO SPAGHETTI

SOY FREE **WHEAT FREE** **RAW**

You'll need a tool to shape the zucchini into spaghetti. If you don't have it, you can make raw lasagna, they taste the same and it's easy to make. You just need to cut your zucchini in wide strips, from top to bottom (a single zucchini should make around five or six strips). Put your strips on the counter, salt a little, and let rest for 30 minutes until they "sweat". Remove the water with a towel and assemble, one layer of zucchini, one of pesto, until you've placed it all. Serves two.

OR LASAGNA

4 medium zucchinis
Pesto:
a bunch of fresh basil
½ cup of almonds
5 sun dried tomatoes, soaked for 10 minutes
Extra virgin olive oil, to taste
2 cloves of garlic

Blend all your ingredients in a food processor.
Mix into your raw spaghetti/lasagna. Add a little bit of extra virgin olive
oil. You shouldn't need salt, as the sun dried tomatoes are already salty.
To serve, put on a flat serving tray, and decorate with some basil leaves
and some chopped almonds or pinenuts.

Rigatoni with Red Bell Pepper Cream

2 cloves garlic
3 medium red bell peppers
½ tsp chili flakes
1 bunch fresh parsley
olive oil
½ cup non-dairy milk
salt
pepper
¼ cup almonds (optional)
18 ounces (or 500 grams) rigatoni

Put the water on to boil. Meanwhile, in a pan, heat the olive oil, the garlic cloves, and the chili. Sauté one minute and add the pepper, roughly chopped in chunks. Let cook for about 15 minutes on high heat, until the pepper is tender. Let cool a little and blend together with the non-dairy milk. Add salt and pepper.
Serve mixed in with the pasta and with some fresh parsley to decorate.
Optional: grind some toasted almonds really fine and serve on top.

Tomato Creamy Lo's Pasta

This is my little brother's favorite pasta and is so simple.
He is more and more conscious about what he eats and
I can support his effort by making this pasta!

2 cloves garlic, minced
bit of fresh basil, chopped
olive oil
6.7 liquid ounces (or 200ml) non-dairy cream
3 cup fresh diced tomatoes
18 ounces (or 500 grams) spaghetti or bucatini

Sauté the garlic in olive oil, add the basil and the tomatoes and cook on
medium heat until they are tender.
This recipe is all about the tomatoes,
so their quality really makes the difference.
Add half of the cream, stir a little and remove from the stove.
Mix in with the cooked pasta
and add the remaining cream before serving.

CURRIED ZUCCHINI CARROTS PASTA

SOY FREE

One of my roommates from a long time ago used to make pasta like this. I never got the recipe from her but this is how I remember it, and it's easy and quick to prepare.

3 carrots
3 zucchinis
4 cloves garlic, crushed
2 Tbsp Indian curry powder
½ tsp turmeric
salt
olive oil
18 ounces (or 500 grams) short pasta

Boil the water for the pasta.
Meanwhile grate the carrot and zucchini.
In a pan with olive oil, sauté the crushed garlic
and add the veggies, then the curry powder and the turmeric.
When the pasta is cooked, mix together with the veggies,
adding a little bit of olive oil so it is not too dry.

Red Pesto Pasta

SOY FREE

2 cups sun dried tomatoes (if totally dried soak them in water for ten minutes)
1 bunch fresh basil
¼ cup almonds
1 garlic clove
1 Tbsp olive oil
18 ounces (or 500 grams) short pasta

Put a pot of water on to boil.
Meanwhile put all the ingredients
for the red pesto in a food processor.
Add a little water or oil if too dry,
depending on what kind of sun dried tomatoes you are using.
When the pasta is cooked,
mix together and serve decorated
with a few whole almonds, basil leaves,
and chopped sun dried tomatoes.

Ravioli Spinach Ricotta and Walnuts

Dough:
3 cups white flour
1 tsp salt
1 cup water
¾ cup non-dairy milk
pinch of turmeric

Filling:
2 cloves of garlic
18 ounces (or 500 grams) spinach
1 tsp chili
pinch of nutmeg
½ cup walnuts, chopped
1 ricotta (see recipe pg. 139)
olive oil

Sauce:
5 tomatoes, chopped
2 garlic cloves, whole
1 bunch of fresh basil
1/3 of the ricotta (optional)
olive oil
salt

Mix the dry ingredients for the dough, kneading, and adding slowly the wet ingredients.

The dough should be really soft and elastic—if too dry add a little bit of (non-dairy) milk.

Put in plastic wrap and let rest for half an hour in the fridge.

Meanwhile, prepare the filling. Make the ricotta according to the recipe. In a pan, heat a little bit of olive oil and sauté the garlic and chili. Add the spinach (boiled if fresh, or thawed if frozen) and cook a few minutes. Season with salt and a little bit of nutmeg and then blend in a food processor. Put the spinach filling in a bowl and add the chopped nuts and 2/3 of the ricotta.

Put some water to boil in a big pan. Start preparing the ravioli, rolling the dough as thin as possible on the counter. This is really important as thin dough makes the ravioli taste so much better. Cut squares of equal sizes and put a spoon of filling on one, closing it on top with another square of dough. Press the edges of the ravioli with a fork so it is sealed and won't open while cooking. Repeat this process until the dough is gone.

When the water is boiling, add some salt and put a few ravioli in at a time. When they float they are ready to be scooped out. Cook all the ravioli this way, making sure that when you take them out you put them on a tray one next to each other, not on top, otherwise they will stick together.

When they are all boiled, prepare the tomato sauce by heating a little bit of olive oil in a pan and adding the garlic cloves. Add a little chopped basil, then the tomatoes, and cook on medium heat for a few minutes until the tomatoes become liquid. Add the remaining ricotta or keep it like that. Add the ravioli in the pan and slightly cook them in the sauce on low heat, just so they infuse with the flavor. Serve hot with a little basil on top.

Pasta Broccoli Potatoes and Walnuts

SOY FREE

2 broccoli heads
3 cups cubed potatoes
2 garlic cloves
2 tsp chili flakes
¼ cup crushed walnuts
salt
black pepper
vegetable stock
olive oil
18 ounces (or 500 gr) short pasta

In a big pot, bring some water and stock to boil.
Meanwhile, chop the broccoli into small pieces,
keeping only the heads, and cube the potatoes.
When the water is boiling, put them together in it.
Let the broccoli cook for five minutes and the potatoes for ten.
Don't drain the water, as it is also used for the pasta.
It will be easy to take the broccoli out as they stay at the surface.
Heat a little olive oil in a pan
Add the minced garlic as well as the chili flakes.
Add the potatoes and broccoli and put on low heat.
Stir a little bit so that everything gets well mixed,
then with a potato masher gently mash
so that the potatoes break and form a sort of cream around the broccoli.
Add the walnuts to the sauce.
Season with salt and pepper and mix in with the cooked pasta.
Decorate with a few walnuts on top.

ASPARAGUS CREAM LASAGNA

Cream:
4 bunches of asparagus
1 cup non-dairy milk
2 cloves garlic
salt
pepper
lasagna sheets
(precooking is quicker, otherwise we need to boil them)
1 bechamelle (see recipe pg. 138)

Preheat the oven at 400° F.
Cut the asparagus into sticks,
removing only the very end of the asparagus,
where it is really hard.
Boil the asparagus until tender, then drain.
Let cool a little bit
Blend in a food processor with all ingredients until it's creamy.
The cream shouldn't be too runny.

Lightly grease a baking pan and put on a layer of lasagna sheets.
Add the asparagus cream and some bechamelle on top.
Repeat until you use up your ingredients.
The last layer should be bechamelle.
Bake for about 45 minutes.

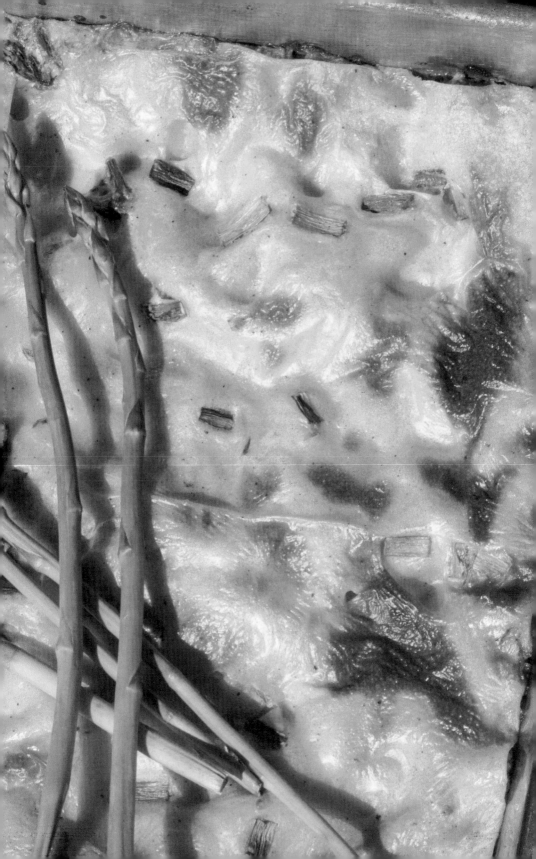

Chickpeas are a great meat substitute, both for their flavor and texture, and they are rich in proteins and therefore very nourishing. My boyfriend told me how to do this ragu, which means "meat sauce."

TOMATO LASAGNA WITH CHICKPEA "RAGU"

Sauce:
5 garlic cloves, minced
1 white onion, chopped
1 ½ cups cooked chickpeas, mashed
¼ cup white wine
olive oil
20 tomatoes, chopped
fresh basil

1 bechamelle (see recipe pg. 138)
lasagna sheets
1 eggplant (optional)
1 zucchini (optional)

Preheat the oven at 400° F.
If you want to add them in the lasagna, slice the eggplant and zucchini lengthwise. Let them rest with a little salt on them until they sweat their water out. Remove with a cloth and grill in the oven or in a pan, or even better—on a grill. Put aside.

In a pan, heat the olive oil, the garlic,
the onion, and part of the fresh basil.
Sauté a few minutes, then add the chickpeas and the wine.
After two or three minutes,
add the tomatoes, and cook on medium heat
until the tomatoes are totally cooked and are liquid.

In a square baking pan, put a layer of the tomato sauce then some lasagna sheets. Cover with more tomato sauce and some bechamelle. Repeat until you finish the ingredients, the last layer being tomato sauce and bechamelle.
Bake for about 45 minutes.

Spaghetti Garlic Chili and Oil

SOY FREE

As the title says, this is a garlic and chili pasta, so feel free to add as much as you like… it is really simple and good to make when in a hurry. I've added a second version if you want to be a little more creative and have excess seitan to use.

Version 1:

½ garlic bulb

1 Tbsp chili flakes

olive oil

pepper

nutritional yeast.

18 ounces (or 500 gr) spaghetti

Cook the pasta al dente, taking it out one minute before it's finished. Meanwhile in a pan, sauté the minced garlic and the chili in the olive oil until very fragrant. When the pasta is cooked, drain and add to the pan. Cook on low heat for about one minute, and then serve with pepper and nutritional yeast on top.

Version 2:

(Add minced seitan to it)

1 seitan recipe (see recipe pg. 104)

¼ cup white wine

4 Tbsp tomato passata (paste)

½ garlic bulb

1 Tbsp chili flakes

olive oil

pepper

nutritional yeast

Cook the seitan according to the recipe. When the broth is almost absorbed, drain the seitan chunks and let them cool. When they are cool enough, process them in the food processor until minced. In a pan with a little olive oil, sauté the garlic and chili until fragrant on medium heat. Add the minced seitan and sauté a minute, then add the wine. Stir a little, then add the tomato passata and cook for about ten minutes, stirring so it doesn't stick to the bottom of the pan. Mix the cooked pasta in the pan, cook for a minute and serve topped with pepper and nutritional yeast.

MAIN DISHES

Leftover risotto is one
of the best ways to make rice balls.
You might need to take the big pieces of veggies
out if they are too big. Take a handful of rice,
roll it into a ball shape, and then roll it into
nutritional yeast or breadcrumbs. Fry in a pan
with olive oil, turning it to cook evenly. It
tastes delicious and is really easy to make.

GARDEN RISOTTO

SOY FREE **WHEAT FREE**

5 big mushrooms, chopped
3 small bell peppers, one of each color, chopped
1 cup cubed pumpkin
½ cup fried eggplant
1 bunch fresh spinach
½ onion, chopped
2 garlic cloves, minced
fresh parsley
salt
pepper
3 cups risotto rice
broth
½ cup white wine (optional)
olive oil

Cut the eggplants into strips and fry them in a pan with olive oil. Put aside. Prepare the broth with hot water. In a big pot, sauté the onion and garlic. Add the mushrooms, peppers, and pumpkin and cook a few minutes. Add the rice and sauté a few minutes, stirring continuously. Add the wine if you're using it and stir for another couple of minutes, until the rice has changed color and is whiter. Cover with the broth and turn to low heat. It can take quite some time to cook the rice but this way it tastes better, as the vegetables release all of their flavors. Stir continuously, add some broth as it evaporates. The risotto is ready when the rice is cooked and creamy. Season with salt and pepper and garnish with the eggplants, some fresh chopped spinach, and parsley.
Serve right away or if you want to serve it later, add a little broth and cook for a few minutes to reheat.

Veggie Gateau

SOY FREE   WHEAT FREE

I ate a version of this at one of my mum's friend's house and it was surprisingly vegan and delicious. They didn't know I was coming over for dinner and I thought I wouldn't have anything to eat but it turned out that almost the whole meal was vegan, and it is such a rare thing in France that I thought I should thank them by putting this dish in here. You can vary as much as you want with the veggies to use, depending on the season. It always tastes good and looks beautiful!

4 potatoes
7 tomatoes
2 zucchini
olive oil
mixed herbs
salt
pepper

Preheat the oven at 400° F. Slice all of the veggies really thin. It's easier if you have a slicer for the potatoes and the zucchini but you can also do it by hand, as long as the slices are thin. Grease a round cake pan with olive oil and start layering the veggies. Every third layer should be a tomato one, with mixed herbs, salt, and olive oil on top. Finish with a layer of tomatoes, add the herbs, salt, pepper and a little olive oil, and bake covered for about 45 minutes to one hour (depending on the size of the slices and how many layers, the more you have the more they'll need to cook). Remove the lid and serve.

POTATO CROQUETTES

SOY FREE **WHEAT FREE**

35 ounces (or 1 kg) potatoes, peeled or washed
1 Tbsp margarine
1 or 2 Tbsp non-dairy milk
¼ cup nutritional yeast
salt
pepper
oregano
bread crumbs

Boil the potatoes until tender. Drain and let cool, then mash with the margarine and the milk. Add the nutritional yeast, salt and pepper to taste, and some oregano. Shape them like a football and roll them into the breadcrumbs (or nutritional yeast for gluten free, in that case put a little less in the potatoes). Fry them in a pan with olive oil on both sides.

Onion Pie

For the crust I follow my mum's recipe for her pesto tomato pie
(which is delicious)

1 cup whole wheat flour
1 1/3 cup white flour
½ cup olive oil
½ cup water
1 tsp baking powder (optional)
salt

Knead all to form a ball.
Place in the fridge in a plastic bag and let rest for half an hour.

Filling:
6 white onions
olive oil
salt
1 bechamelle recipe (see recipe pg. 138)

Preheat the oven on 375° F.
Chop the onions and cook them in a pan with olive oil until caramelized.
Season with salt, then add the bechamelle and cook on low heat for two
or three minutes, until it thickens a little. Roll the dough on a floured
surface and put it in a greased pie pan. With a fork, make some holes on
the bottom to release trapped air when it cooks. Make sure that there is
enough dough on the side so the filling doesn't go overboard. Pour the
onion filling in and bake for 30 minutes or until the crust is brownish. Let
cool so the pie can set, and serve lukewarm.

Quinoa Potato and Shitake

> 2 cups quinoa cooked in 4 cups water with broth
> 3 ½ cups diced potatoes
> 2 cups chopped shitake mushrooms, dried or fresh
> 2 garlic cloves
> hazelnut or walnut oil
> salt
> pepper
> mixed herbs: thyme, rosemary, marjoram

Put the water and quinoa into a pot with a lid. When the water is boiling, lower the heat and simmer for 15 or 20 minutes, until the water evaporates totally and the quinoa "breaks," so that you can see the little white circle on the seeds.

Meanwhile, prepare the potatoes and mushrooms. If using dried shitake, soak them in hot water for five minutes, then drain. Dice the potatoes really small without peeling them and chop the mushrooms in a food processor so they are in tiny pieces. In a pan, heat the oil and the whole garlic cloves. Add the herbs then the potatoes and cook for five minutes, until the potatoes start to be a little crunchy. Add the mushrooms and cook for another two or three minutes. Add a little water and cook until the potatoes are tender. Mix with the cooked quinoa, salt, pepper, and a little hazelnut oil.

Quinoa is full of good things
for you. It is often confused as a grain,
but it is actually a seed and therefore is
perfect for people with intolerance to
grains and wheat. It acts as a blood tonic,
helps digestion, is rich in lysine, which is
an essential amino acid; it provides a high
amount of fiber and a good amount of
proteins, as well as a good
source of calcium.

Blend the dry ingredients in a food processor.
Add the liquids, the herbs, and seasoning.
Put in a bowl and mix all the
ingredients until they hold together.
Form some patties about 1/2" / 1 cm thick.
Fry in a pan with vegetable or olive oil,
until each side is brown, about two minutes each.
Makes about 25 patties.

Gluten Free Burgers

WHEAT FREE

1 cup cooked chickpeas
½ carrot
1 celery stick
1 white onion
2 garlic cloves
1 cup TVP, rehydrated
9 ounces (or 250 grams) tofu
5 mushrooms
½ cup walnuts
3 tsp mixed herbs
1 tsp liquid smoke
5 Tbsp soy sauce
¼ cup nutritional yeast
2 tsp Dijon mustard
2 Tbsp tomato paste
2 Tbsp barbecue sauce
1 tsp garlic powder

POTATO PATTIES

> 35 ounces (or 1 kg) potatoes
> 2 white onions
> ¼ cup nutritional yeast
> salt
> pepper
> oil to fry

Grate the potatoes and chop the onions small. Mix in a bowl with the other ingredients. Transfer to a colander as the potatoes lose a lot of water. Form patties in your hand, pressing hard to express all the water. You'll have to repeat that for every patty, otherwise they won't hold together. Fry each side in vegetable oil until golden. These are perfect for breakfast but are also great in buns with tomatoes, veggies, and lettuce. Put a bowl under the colander where you put the grated potatoes and onions. When you are done with the patties, pour out the water. On the bottom of the bowl there will be all the starch from the potatoes, a thick, white layer. You can keep it and use it to thicken a sauce, just like you would with cornstarch.

Potatoes and Carrots Puree with Caramelized Onions

WHEAT FREE

5 carrots
10 medium or big potatoes
1/3 cup non-dairy milk
3 Tbsp margarine
salt
black pepper
vegetable stock
3 red onions
1 tsp raw sugar
½ tsp salt
2 Tbsp balsamic vinegar
olive oil

Peel and cut the carrots. In a pot, bring water to a boil, add some stock, and put the carrots in. Peel the potatoes and add to the pot. Let them cook until both the carrots and the potatoes are tender. Meanwhile, heat some olive oil in a pan. Slice the onions and sauté in the pan until they start changing color. Add the sugar, salt, and balsamic vinegar and cook a few more minutes, stirring so they don't burn. When the potatoes and carrots are cooked, drain and transfer to a bowl. Add the margarine, milk, salt, and pepper and mash by hand or with an electrical hand blender, depending on the consistency you prefer. Serve with the caramelized onions on top.

SAMOSAS

Samosas are good for leftovers. I usually make them after a curry: I drain the liquid and put the filling in a food processor, adding a few spring onions or anything…They are really good with the massaman tofu mushroom soup filling. The day after the soup, drain the liquid, keeping it aside (you can cook the rice in it for example, or if it's not much, add to a fried rice or fried noodles). Blend the remaining tofu and mushrooms coarsely, adding some green onions and a little soy sauce. The filling is ready!

For the dough:
3 cups white flour
1 1/2 cup water
1 Tbsp sesame seeds
1 pinch turmeric
pinch of salt
oil to deep fry

Mix the dry ingredients together. Slowly add the oil and the water to form a soft dough. Knead until you can form a ball. Let rest for about 30 minutes. When ready, cut the dough in half and roll it in a rectangle shape, quite thin. Cut some squares out of it and put a spoon of filling in the middle of each. Close the square with the top part coming over the filling and the edge sticking together. You can either seal it with a fork, or make some little "rolls." Deep fry for a few minutes. Makes about 25 medium-small samosas.

Cannellini al Fiasco

SOY FREE **WHEAT FREE**

2 cup cannellini beans
2 celery stalks, chopped
1 big carrot, chopped
2 garlic cloves, whole
1 bunch rosemary
1 bay leaf
vegetable stock
salt
black pepper
olive oil

Soak the beans overnight. In the morning, rinse, put in a pot with broth to cover the beans, and bring to a boil with a lid on. When the water is boiling, take the lid off and simmer for about an hour. In a pan, heat some olive oil, garlic, celery, carrot, and rosemary for a few minutes. Add to the beans and stir. Add the bay leaf and cook on medium heat for another hour, making sure that there is always enough water to cover the beans. The beans are ready when the stew does not contain too much liquid, and is creamy. Add salt and pepper and serve warm, removing the bay leaf.

Make your own vegetable stock with a carrot, a small potato, two celery sticks with their leaves, onion, garlic, and some fresh herbs, all unpeeled. Bring to a boil and then simmer for 45 minutes. Remove the veggies.

Pumpkin Gnocchi

For the gnocchi:
2 cups pumpkin, boiled
2 medium potatoes
2 cups white flour,
plus a little to knead with
salt

For the sauce:
2 Tbsp margarine
1 tsp sage

Boil the potatoes and blend the pumpkin into a puree. Mix it with flour and form a soft dough. Divide in four parts. Roll each part into a sausage, about 1 1/4" thick. Slice little gnocchi out of the roll, about 1/2" / 1 cm. Put them on a lightly floured tray and boil some water. When the water is boiling, start dropping the gnocchi in. They are ready when they float to the surface. Take them out and place them on a tray. When they are all ready, on medium heat, melt the margarine and the sage in a pan. Add the gnocchi and mix well until coated. Add salt if needed and serve straight away.

There are many ways to do gnocchi. This is just a version of them but you can get really creative and vary the consistency of the dough if you want them softer or harder; you can vary the sauces and serve them with a pesto, or a tomato sauce... just explore!

MOMOKO'S JAPANESE CURRY

My friend Tomoko is a wonderful cook
and she taught me a few Japanese dishes that were not maki,
Japanese pancakes, or tempura. Everyone loved this creamy curry,
so she wanted to share the recipe in this book.

5 carrots
5 onions
5 potatoes
3 broccoli heads
10 Tbsp flour
10 fluid ounces (or 300 ml) soy milk
5 Tbsp Indian curry powder (spicy if you like)
3 Tbsp margarine
1 tsp salt

Chop the veggies in big chunks. Sauté the onions in a pan with oil then add the other veggies. Slowly add water to cover and cook the veggies until tender. Meanwhile, in a small bowl, mix the flour, curry powder, and soy milk. When boiling, add the mixture to the pan and slowly stir. Turn the heat to medium and cook until the curry gets thicker. If you want, you can add a little bit of margarine to make it creamier. Serve with rice.

SAVORY FILLED CRÊPES

Crêpes:
2 ½ cups flour
4 cups water
salt
pinch turmeric
margarine, to cook with

Filling:
2 medium zucchini, diced
5 mushrooms, chopped small
1 bunch arugula
2 garlic cloves, minced.
fresh parsley
½ Veg Ricotta (for recipe see pg. 139 or use 100 gr cream cheese)
¼ cup crushed walnuts
olive oil
salt
pepper

Topping:
1 bechamelle recipe (for recipe see pg. 138)
nutritional yeast flakes

Vigorously stir all of the crêpe ingredients. Let it rest in the fridge for half an hour. Meanwhile, prepare the filling. Heat a pan with olive oil and sauté the garlic, then add the zucchini. Cook a few minutes then add the mushrooms. After another two or three minutes take it off the stove and add the ricotta (or cream cheese) and the walnuts. Mix well and add salt and pepper.

Start making the crepes, heating a little margarine in a pan. Make sure they are not too thick; half a scoop of the batter should be sufficient. Heat on both sides but do not over-cook as they will cook in the oven too. Preheat the oven on 375° F. When all the crepes are done, put a scoop of filling in the middle of each, one after another, adding the arugula on top, and roll to close. Put in a lightly greased pan. Make bechamelle—you can add a few Tbsp of milk so it's not too dense as it will harden in the oven. Pour over the crepes, sprinkle some nutritional yeast and bake for about twenty minutes.

Veggie Fritti

SOY FREE

These are the Italian version of vegetable tempura. It's similar to the Japanese version, although the batter differs a little. It's really big around Christmas and New Year and is usually eaten as antipasti, but it doesn't really matter…

Batter:
1 ½ cups white flour
2 ¼ cup water, cold
pinch of sweet paprika
pinch of oregano
salt
pepper

Veggies:
Artichokes, eggplants, peppers, mushrooms, onions, sometimes apples

Chop the vegetables into square chunks.
Dip them in the batter and then deep fry!

Roasted Potatoes, Mushrooms, and Green Beans in White Wine

SOY FREE

WHEAT FREE

1 dozen mushrooms
8 potatoes
18 ounces (or 500 grams) green beans, boiled in water or veggie stock
5 cloves garlic or 1 red onion, chopped
½ cup white wine
¼ cup olive oil
salt
pepper
thyme

Mix all the ingredients in a tray and put in the oven at 400° F.
Cook until roasted.

PARMIGIANA

2 big eggplants
½ white onion
2 garlic cloves
fresh basil
35 ounces (or 1 kg) tomatoes
olive oil
1 bechamelle (see recipe pg. 138)

Preheat the oven to 400° F. Cut the eggplants lengthwise in slices about 1/2" / 1 cm thick. Place them on a counter and sparkle some salt on them. This will make them "sweat" after 10 minutes or so. With a cloth, absorb the water
. Grill them in a pan with no oil or on a grill; I feel fried eggplants are too heavy. This way you can have seconds without dying! Make the tomato sauce by heating the garlic, onion, and basil in the olive oil. Add the tomatoes (roughly chopped) and let cook on medium heat until the tomatoes start to form a sauce. With a hand blender, blend the sauce and then season. Make the bechamelle. Put a little tomato sauce in a square tray. You can start layering the parmigiana, with one layer of eggplants, one of tomato sauce and one of bechamelle. Do two or more layers, finishing with the bechamelle and if you want, sprinkle a little nutritional yeast. Put in the oven and bake for 45 minutes. You can let it cool a little so it sets and then reheat (it's actually really good the day after!) or serve

Mini Forest Pies

SOY FREE

Crust:
1 cup whole wheat flour
1 1/3 cups white flour
½ cup olive oil
½ cup water
1 Tbsp flaxseeds

Filling:
1 leek
4 tomatoes
1 zucchini
1 carrot
½ red bell pepper
½ green bell pepper
5 mushrooms
mixed herbs: fresh parsley, thyme, basil
¼ cup white wine
olive oil
salt

Knead the ingredients for the crust, form a ball, and put in the fridge to rest for half an hour in a plastic bag or wrap (I don't like to waste wrap so I usually put it in a resealable plastic bag). Preheat the oven to 375° F. Meanwhile prepare the filling. Chop the veggies in tiny little squares, as small as possible. In a pan, heat the olive oil and the leek. Add the herbs and sauté a few minutes. Add the rest of the vegetables and bathe with the white wine. Cook for about ten minutes on medium heat, then remove from the stove. Season. Take the dough from the fridge and roll onto a floured surface. With a mug or a cookie cutter, cut some circles out—the size of muffins. Grease a muffin tray and put each circle in each muffin case. Spoon some filling in and bake until the crust is golden, about 25 minutes. Makes about 15 mini pies.

Potato Taro Cauliflower Coconut Gratin

WHEAT FREE

½ head cauliflower
8 potatoes
2 taro roots
1 coconut bechamelle (see recipe pg. 138)
nutritional yeast
salt
pepper

Chop the cauliflower, potatoes, and taro in big chunks and put in a baking tray, slightly greased with a little margarine. Add a little salt and pepper and then cover with the coconut bechamelle and sprinkle with nutritional yeast. Bake at 400° F for about 45 minutes, until the top is little roasted.

For the coconut bechamelle, use the traditional bechamelle recipe but instead of using all soy milk, use half coconut milk and half soy milk

Potato Salad with Paprika Tofu-Mayo

WHEAT FREE

35 ounces (or 1 kg) potatoes
½ cup olive oil
2 lemons juiced
¼ cup apple cider vinegar
½ cup nutritional yeast
2 Tbsp smoked paprika
2 Tbsp Dijon mustard
fresh parsley
small bell pepper (different color, 1/3 each)
1 small broccoli head
¾ cup pine nuts roasted on the stove
salt and pepper

Peel and chop the potatoes in squares. Boil for about 25 minutes, until the potatoes are tender but not falling apart. Drain and put them in a big salad bowl.
In a medium bowl, vigorously stir the olive oil, the lemon juice, the vinegar, the nutritional yeast, the mustard, and the smoked paprika. Chop the broccoli and bell peppers really small and add to the sauce. Pour over the potatoes, adding the roasted pine nuts and the parsley. Toss well evenly and put in the fridge at least 2 hours until the potatoes are cool. Serve with the mayo on the side.

For the tofu mayo:
1 small tofu block
1 garlic clove
1 lemon, juiced
water
1 pinch of paprika
fresh basil
salt

Blend all until really creamy.

Seitan in Red Wine Sauce

It took me a while to make some good seitan, because I was never happy with the recipes I had. I figured out that slow and low heat cooking is the best if you want a nice texture, so it takes me five hours to make this, but it is worth it. Other ways of cooking seitan: steaming and baking, and it can come out really nice too, but that is a little bit more complicated, so this is a good recipe for a beginner.

For the seitan:

1 ½ cup wheat gluten
1 tsp sage
1 tsp thyme
½ tsp garlic powder
2 ½ Tbsp garlic powder
1 Tbsp tomato paste
1 ¼ cup water

Mix all the dry ingredients. Slowly add the wet ingredients and knead into dough. The dough should be quite elastic and not too dry—if needed, add a tablespoon of water at a time to reach the desired consistency. Form a ball with the dough and let it rest for a couple of minutes, while you prepare the broth.

Broth:

water
soy sauce
2 bay leaves
celery seeds (optional)
garlic
onion

Prepare the broth as you like it the most. The only important thing is to have enough liquid in the pan, because the seitan is going to expand quite a lot, so calculate at least twice as much as you would put for the size of your dough. Put on the stove on high heat.

Cut the seitan dough in four. Form a roll from each piece and cut some chunks out of it, about 1 1/4" / 3 cm long. Don't put the chunks on top of each other as they are gonna stick; separate them on a tray. Put the seitan chunks in the broth, cover, and let boil. When the broth is boiling, turn the heat to low and let cook for an hour and a half, without the lid so the broth can evaporate. Drain the seitan, keeping the broth aside (you can re-use it to cook).

Prepare the sauce:
Olive oil
1/2 cup of red wine
1/2 cup of tomato sauce
2 or 3 carrots
3 celery stalks
bunch fresh herbs (basil, parsley, sage, rosemary)
2 small white onions
2 garlic cloves, minced
½ chili, minced

Heat the olive oil in a wide pan. Add the onions, garlic, and herbs. Sauté a few minutes on high heat then add the chili, the carrots, and celery. Sauté for another few minutes, until the whole room smells like Heaven. At this point, add the seitan chunks; if you feel they are too big you can cut them in half before putting them in the pan. Reduce the heat to low and add half a cup of red wine, a little bit of broth, and a half cup of tomato sauce. Now the important part is to let the seitan soak up the sauce, so the more you cook, the better it will taste. I usually cook it like that for two to three hours, adding a little more broth once in a while and stirring to make sure it doesn't stick to the bottom. The seitan is ready when it is turning brown and most of the sauce has evaporated. Serve as a main dish with potatoes, or rice, or steamed vegetables....

Careful! A lot of wines use isinglass (fish), eggs, or milk in the filtering process and therefore are not vegan. I know it sounds crazy to put fish, milk, or eggs in wine—but this shows how powerful the fish and dairy industry is. Animal by-products are in a lot of random stuff!

SEITAN SCHNITZELS

SOY FREE

Schnitzel seems hard to make and easy to buy already made; but they are actually quite simple to make, if you have a little patience. Make the seitan as explained above, except instead of cutting the dough into chunks, you want to cut it in bigger pieces, the shape of a schnitzel. Keep in mind that seitan expands while cooking so don't make the pieces too big. Once they've cooked in the broth until it has almost evaporated, drain the seitan and prepare the batter for the schnitzel.

Seitan:

2 cups wheat gluten

1 ½ cups water

2 Tbsp tomato paste

¼ cup nutritional yeast

mixed herbs: thyme, sage

garlic powder

1 ½ cups white flour

2 ½ cups water

salt

pepper

breadcrumbs

oil to fry

lemon wedges to serve

fresh parsley to decorate

Dip each schnitzel in the batter and then in the breadcrumbs. The batter should be quite runny, not too dense. Fry on each side in a pan with oil for a few minutes until golden brown. Serve with some lemon juice sprinkled on top and some lemon wedges on the side.

Free the Beef Bourguignon Stew

1 seitan recipe (see recipe pg. 106)
6 carrots, sliced
1 onion
2 garlic cloves, whole
15 button mushrooms, cut in half
18 liquid ounces (or ½ lt) red wine
2 cups tomato paste
1 cup or more broth
margarine

Cook your seitan in a broth for two hours. Drain, keeping the remaining broth aside. In a pot, heat a little bit of margarine and sauté the chopped onion and the garlic cloves. Add the seitan and cook on medium or high heat for a few minutes. Add the carrots and the mushrooms, stir well, and cook another two minutes. At this point add all the liquid, which should almost cover the seitan and the veggies, but not totally. Put a lid on, bring to a boil, then reduce to low heat and simmer for about two hours, stirring once in a while. The stew shouldn't dry out, so add a little broth if needed. Serve over steamed potatoes.

SPINACH QUICHE

1 crust recipe (see the one used in the onion pie recipe pg. 76)
35 ounces (or 1 kg) fresh spinach
nutmeg
salt
2 garlic cloves
1 or 2 tsp chili flakes
olive oil
a few dried raisins
1 bechamelle (see recipe pg. 138)

Make the crust according to the recipe. Preheat the oven on 375° F. Cook the spinach without water in a pot over high heat. The spinach contains a lot of water and will release naturally.
Drain spinach and press the water out as much as possible.
Heat the olive oil in a pan and sauté the garlic cloves and chili flakes. Add the spinach and cook a couple of minutes. Season with salt and a pinch of nutmeg, then let cool. Blend in a food processor, then put it back in the pan with the bechamelle. Let cook on low heat for a couple of minutes, then add the raisins and mix.

Roll the crust, put in a greased tray, and poke holes in it with a fork to avoid air bubbles. Make sure the sides are high enough. Pour the filling in and cook for about thirty minutes, until the crust is golden. Let cool and serve lukewarm.

SOUPS

Massaman Tofu Mushroom Soup

WHEAT FREE

For the paste:
4 small red chilies

3 small shallots

2 tsp ground cardamom

1 cinnamon stick

1 tsp black peppercorns

1 tsp coriander seeds

1 tsp cumin seeds

1 lime rind and juice

2 garlic cloves

1 stalk lemongrass

In a food processor, reduce all of the ingredients to a paste. You'll only use one fouth cup of the paste for the soup but the paste, if kept in the fridge, can last a few months and be used in curries so it's good to make more than you need so you don't need to do it every time.

For the soup:
½ cup dried shitake mushrooms

2 cups fresh button mushrooms, chopped

2 cans coconut milk

½ block of tofu, cubed

soy sauce

water

Rehydrate the shitakesi want one in hot water for five minutes. Drain and grind in the food processor. Heat the paste in a big pot with a little water or a little oil and sauté a few minutes. Add the shitake and the tofu and fry another few minutes. Add the coconut milk, some water, and bring to a boil. Add the mushrooms, some soy sauce, and bring to medium heat. Cook until the mushrooms become smaller, about twenty minutes. Serve with some rice noodles or rice.

Spinach Gazpacho

SOY FREE   **WHEAT FREE**   **RAW**

½ cucumber, peeled
1 red bell pepper
5 tomatoes
5 garlic cloves
7 ounces (or 200 grams) spinach
1/4 cup extra virgin olive oil
1 Tbsp wine vinegar
salt

Blend all the ingredients until smooth and creamy. You might want to blend the first half of the spinach and add the rest later, as they take up quite a lot of space.

Careful! When you buy garlic, make sure not to buy the totally white ones, usually called "chinese garlic." It is bleached to get the white color and contains of lot of nasty chemicals to make it last longer.

SALMOREJO

This is a cold soup from a town I used to live in, Cordoba, in Spain. Andalusia is not really veg-friendly. If you have to eat out, this is probably the only popular vegan dish, as long as you stop them from serving it topped with ham or eggs. But the soup itself is totally vegan, so if you travel there you can eat salmorejo a gogo—I never got tired of it.

6 tomatoes
1 small red bell pepper
3 ½ ounces (or 100 grams) old bread, hard, soaked in water then drained
5 cloves garlic
1/8 cup extra virgin olive oil
salt

Blend all until creamy. It is similar to gazpacho, although you can taste the difference. Eat cold.

CARROT SOUP

This is a really quick and easy soup to make.

35 ounces (or 1 kg) carrots
2 medium potatoes
a little olive oil
fresh parsley
salt
pepper
broth

Heat the olive oil or the margarine in a pot on high heat. Add the carrots peeled and roughly chopped into chunks. Cook for a few minutes, then cover with broth. Peel and chop the potatoes and add to the soup. Cook until the veggies are tender, about half an hour. Blend with a hand blender; if you want it to be really creamy, blend it for a while. The soup should be quite thick, not runny, although still liquid. Season with salt and pepper. Add some fresh chopped parsley on top. Serve it with caramelized onions on the side.

Miso Soup

WHEAT FREE

¼ leek
½ Tbsp grated ginger
¾ cup grated daikon
¼ cup minced shitake mushrooms
1/8 cup shredded nori seaweed
½ cup grated carrot
1 cup sweet potatoes, cubed
1 cup pumpkin, cubed
1 cup tofu, cubed
½ cup shredded white cabbage, optional
soy sauce, mushroom soy sauce, or water
2 Tbsp miso
little oil, optional

In a big pot, fry the leek, ginger, daikon, carrot, nori, and shitake together, in a little oil or water. Add the tofu and stir for a minute. Add some water and the cubed sweet potatoes and pumpkin and season with soy sauce (if you have vegetarian mushroom soy sauce, you can add a little bit of that too). Cover with a lid, bring to a boil then reduce heat and let cook until the veggies are tender.
Take some liquid from the soup,
put it in a bowl with the miso,
and stir to dissolve the miso.
Put it back into the soup, stir a little bit,
and serve.

BREAD

BRUSCHETTE

SOY FREE

This recipe comes from a friend in Hobart, who got it from a friend, who got it from a friend. I made a few changes so it's easier. It is worth sharing as it is a healthy and tasty bread that is perfect for brushcette or to simply eat as a toast, or as a "scarpetta," which is the term we use in Italy for the bread used to eat the remaining sauce on your plate after you finished your pasta!

You need a heavy-bottom pan with a lid for this recipe.

3 cups of white flour
3 cups of whole wheat flour
½ tsp instant dry yeast
30 fluid ounces (or 900 ml) warm water
2 tsp salt

Mix the ingredients in a bowl with a spatula.
The dough should be sticky, not runny as a
cake batter, but still wet, holding together.
Cover with a plastic wrap and let rise
in a warm place for sixteen to twenty-four
hours. When your dough is ready,
preheat the oven at 450° F / 250° C
with the heavy bottom pan inside.
With the spatula, stir the dough a little.
When the oven has reached the right temperature,
carefully remove the pan, pour the dough in,
and put the lid back on before putting back in the oven.
Cook for about forty-five minutes.

This slow fermentation process makes the bread taste more like a sourdough, and is definitely healthier than quick white bread, using less yeast, no sugar, and no oil.

To make the bruschetta, let the bread cool down and then cut a slice. Toast it a few minutes, then rub with a clove of garlic without removing its skin, just use the bottom. Add extra virgin olive oil and salt, or tapenade, or fresh chopped tomatoes and basil, and enjoy!

FOCACCIA/PIZZA

SOY FREE

In Italy you can have either crunchy focaccia or soft. If you want crunchy, roll the dough really thin and bake until golden, just before burnt. The second way is good if you want to make sandwiches. Cut the focaccia in four pieces and halve each one so you can fill it with whatever filling you like. Two suggestions: tomato basil and olive oil, or the naughty one, Tofutti, wholegrain mustard, seitan slices, and caramelized onions....

Dough:
6 cups all purpose flour
2 ½ cup warm water
2 tsp instant dry yeast
1 ½ tsp malt syrup or sugar
1 tsp salt
¼ cup olive oil
flour to knead

Mix all the dry ingredients in a bowl. Add the wet and knead gently until a ball forms. The dough has to be soft and elastic. Put it in a bowl with flour and cover with a tea towel; let rise for an hour in a warm place. Preheat your oven at 400° F. Cut the dough in three or four pieces. Roll the dough on a floured surface, about a half inch / 1 cm thick. Let the unbaked focaccia rise for about ten minutes. Add olive oil, salt, and rosemary on top of it and bake for fifteen minutes, until slightly golden. Divide in pieces and eat warm. You can vary the topping as much as you like: oregano, thyme, chili oil, and so on.

Ever thought of chocolate pizza?
Each time I say I'm gonna make it, people
make a weird face, like "come on, pizza can't have
chocolate in it!" It turns out that it is a Roman
speciality, and if you think about it, it is just like
bread with a chocolate spread, which doesn't sound
that weird anymore. In Rome, they use nutella to
make it and the spread is usually inside the pizza, like
a sandwich. You can make your own spread or use
some vegan chocolate spread and put it on
your baked dough. It tastes good,
you can't argue about that!

Garlic Scrolls

Dough:
4 cups white flour, plus extra to knead

1 ½ tsp instant yeast

1 tsp sugar

1 tsp salt

¼ cup oil

2 cups lukewarm water

Filling:
6 garlic cloves

12 Tbsp margarine

2 Tbsp mixed herbs

Mix the dry ingredients for the dough in a bowl. Slowly add the wet ingredients and knead for five minutes, until the dough is soft and you can form a ball. Put a towel on it to cover and let it rest in a warm place for one hour. The dough should double in size; however it varies depending on the temperature of the room; the warmer it is, the quicker the dough rises. Meanwhile, prepare the garlic butter. Crush the garlic and mix it, along with the herbs, into the margarine with a fork. Preheat your oven to 400° F. Divide the dough in two. Roll the first piece into a rectangle about 1/4" / 1/2 cm thick. Spread half of the garlic butter evenly over the rectangle. Start to roll the rectangle from the top to the bottom, obtaining a big long roll. Cut in scrolls about 2" / 5 cm wide. Put the scrolls onto a tray with parchment paper and flatten them a little so they look like snails. Bake for twenty-five minutes, until golden brown and the whole kitchen smells like garlic. Makes about fifteen scrolls.

With the same dough you can make some Vegemite rolls, a good savory snack. When you roll the dough into a rectangle, spread a layer of margarine then a mite spread and follow the same process as the garlic scrolls. You can eat it with avocado and tomato salad, for example.

Pizza Crackers

SOY FREE · WHEAT FREE · RAW

1 cup flaxseed
2 cups water
3 grated carrots (I use half orange, half purple carrots)
2 garlic cloves
½ red onion
½ red bell pepper
¼ lemon, juiced
fresh parsley
pinch of cayenne pepper
½ cup of your favorite nuts
3 portobello mushrooms
1/3 cup sun dried tomatoes
1 tsp nutritional yeast flakes
1 tsp chia seeds (optional)

Let the flaxseeds and chia seeds soak overnight in a bowl. The morning after, chop all the ingredients really small and grate the carrots. Mix all together in a bowl and add the lemon juice, the cayenne pepper, and the nutritional yeast flakes. Mix with the flaxseed mixture and stir so it is equally distributed. Pour on the trays of a dehydrator and let it dehydrate for eight hours. When they are crunchy, take the layers of crackers and break them into medium large pieces to snack on.

Flaxseed is one of the richest food sources of Omega 3, which is really good for our immune system. Flaxseed is also a great antioxidant, necessary to destroy the free radicals in the body. Flaxseeds are used to treat urinary problems, enrich the blood, correct hypertension, and so on.

Spinach Braid Bread

3 garlic cloves
2 cups spinach, cooked
pinch of salt, nutmeg, black pepper
6 cups white flour
2 cups lukewarm water
1 tsp sugar
2 tsp instant yeast
olive oil

SOY FREE

Blend the spinach in a food processor. Mince the garlic and heat in a pan with olive oil. Add the spinach and cook a few minutes. Season with salt, pepper, and nutmeg.

In a big bowl, mix the flour, sugar, salt, and yeast. Add the water and the spinach and knead, until you can form a soft ball in your hand. Let rise in a bowl lightly oiled for about one hour or until it has doubled in size. Preheat your oven to 400° F. Take the dough and knead it again a few minutes, then on a lightly floured surface, roll it into a thick rectangle. With a knife, cut it in three, but not totally—keep the top of the rectangle together, so every part is still attached at the same base. Take each part and form a braid, and at the end, seal the parts, pressing them together.

Put on a tray with oven paper and bake for about 30 minutes.

DESSERTS

CORDOBES ORANGE DESSERT

SOY FREE **WHEAT FREE** **RAW**

Now it seems that I put olive oil everywhere, even in desserts, but I actually didn't invent that, I promise. It is perfect to finish a meal, especially if it's little heavy.

> 3 oranges
> little olive oil
> cinnamon

Peel the oranges. Cut them in circles that you place on a plate. Drizzle a little olive oil on top and sprinkle some cinnamon. For this recipe, the quality of the olive oil is important, it has to be extra virgin cold pressed.

A variation is to eat the oranges with chocolate. Mix some olive oil, agave, raw cacao powder, and carob powder to make a raw chocolate sauce. I was surprised when I tried it, but it actually works really well together.

Oat Macadamia Chocolate Cookies

These cookies were born as a special treat for a small boat crew that had been out in action for a long time during the Operation No Compromise in Antarctica. The temperature can reach -94° F (-70° C) with the wind blowing and even with special suits on, the people that stay out for a long time need some calories to fight the cold. I changed them slightly over the years, and this might not even be a definitive version. You can skip the macadamia, or add other nuts, or goji berries, or whatever you fancy.

2 cups white flour
1 cup raw sugar
1 tsp baking powder
5 ounces (or 150 grams) rolled oats
¾ cup cocoa powder
pinch of salt
½ cup macadamia nuts
9 ounces (or 250 grams) non-dairy margarine, at room temperature
1 tsp vanilla
5 Tbsp fresh orange juice

Makes about twenty cookies. Preheat your oven to 400° F. In a food processor, crush the macadamia for a few seconds, keeping some big bits. In a big bowl, sift the flour, baking powder, sugar, cocoa powder, and salt. Add the oats and the macadamia and mix with your hands. Add the vanilla and the orange juice, then the margarine, crumbling it slowly with your hands. Mix with the other ingredients until the dough forms a homogenous ball. This can take a few minutes, making sure that all the ingredients are all mixed together well. Form little balls in your hands, and flatten into a disc of about two and a 1/2" / cm in diameter. Bake the cookies for fifteen minutes and cool on a wire rack until the cookies are firm.

Date and Almond Balls

SOY FREE **WHEAT FREE** **RAW**

According to my friend Dan, these almost taste like white chocolate!

2 cups almonds
1 cup dates
3 Tbsp of date cream (¾ cup dates and 1 ¾ cups of water)
5 or 6 Tbsp of agave
pinch of salt
about ½ cup sesame seeds, to roll in

Makes about fifteen balls. Start by making the date cream, blending the dates and water together—this will make more date cream than you need for the recipe, but it's always handy to have some ready made for more raw recipes, as a snack, or to add to your smoothie. In a food processor, grind the almonds into small pieces and put them in a bowl and process the dates. Put all the ingredients in the food processor—the almonds, dates, date paste, salt, and agave and process until it forms a paste. It should not take more than a minute. The paste should be quite wet but easy to make balls out of. Roll them in your hands, and then add the sesame seeds. Refrigerate for half an hour before serving.

Almonds contain a lot of arginine, which is fundamental for cell production, muscle movement and nitrogen elimination. Almonds are a good source of magnesium and potassium—two fundamental minerals for good heart function. Almonds have a lot of medicinal uses, including treatment of asthma, constipation, fluid retention, skin disorders, fatigue, nervous stress, impotency, and much more.

RAISINS SNAILY SNAP

My friend Susan came in the galley while I was making these and said "Snap! They look good!" so I decided to call these frenchy-style pastries Snaily Snap for her.

Dough:
3 cups white flour
½ cup melted margarine
½ cup non-dairy milk
½ cup warm water
2 tsp dry instant yeast
1/3 cup sugar
pinch of salt

Filling:
4 Tbsp cornstarch
5 Tbsp sugar
1 ½ tsp vanilla
2 cups soy milk
¼ cup raisins
drops of rum, to soak raisins in (optional)

Knead the dough until it is soft and let it rise in a bowl for two hours. Prepare your filling by mixing the cornstarch, sugar, vanilla, and one cup of milk until creamy. Simmer on medium heat for a few minutes, then add the rest of the milk and keep stirring until it becomes creamy and thick. This might take a while, up to fifteen minutes, so be patient. Preheat the oven on 400° F. When the dough has doubled in size, cut it in half and extend it on the counter with the roller, shaping it as a rectangle about 1/2" / one cm thick. Put some of the filling on it, spreading it with a brush. Do not over fill it. Add the raisins and start to roll from the top to bottom, lengthwise. When the dough is rolled, cut it in 1 1/2" / 3-4 cm rolls. The filling will go a little at a time, but it doesn't matter, as you'll save it for later. Put each roll on a tray with baking paper and flatten them so they look like snails. Add the remaining filling and bake until golden, about 25 minutes. Makes about twelve buns.

TIRAMISU

This is an easy version of what is possibly the most famous of Italian desserts. The original recipe calls for some kind of cream cheese and is more caloric than this vegan version, which still tastes amazing and makes everyone happy. We used to have a "tirami-thursday" ritual on the Sam, and even if I didn't make it every Thursday, we still had tiramisu quite a few times during the campaign.

11 ounces (or 325 grams) of vegan biscuits, about 30
8 ½ liquid ounces (or 250 ml) of strong coffee
1 ½ Tbsp of cocoa powder
8 Tbsp cornstarch
4 Tbsp sugar
4 cups non-dairy milk
2 tsp vanilla

Make the cream by mixing the cornstarch, sugar, and one cup of milk on the stove on medium heat. Simmer a few minutes and add the rest of the milk; stir until creamy and thick. Soak the biscuits one by one in the coffee for a few seconds, and start a first layer in a square tray. Add one-third of the cream, and sift some cocoa powder on it. Do another two layers of biscuits, cream, and cocoa, finishing with the cocoa powder all over. Refrigerate four hours before serving.

No Bake Choco-Peanut Pie

There are many versions of this kind of pie, and surely I got the inspiration from some cook book or another I had with me.

Filling:
11 ounces (or 350 g) dark chocolate
¼ cup and 6 Tbsp of non-dairy milk
1 ½ cup peanut butter, crunchy
1 can coconut cream, previously put in the fridge a few hours (this helps to have the creamy part separating from the liquid)
½ cup almonds, hazelnut, and raisins mixed
coconut flakes

Crust:
½ pack of digestive biscuits (around 200 grams)
6 Tbsp margarine

Crush the digestive biscuits and the margarine together to form the crust. The easiest way is to use a food processor, as it will take only a few seconds. Press the crust into a round cake tray. Melt the chocolate in a bowl over some water on the stove on medium heat (bain-marie), adding the six tablespoons of non-dairy milk slowly. Stir continuously, being careful not to overcook the chocolate. When the chocolate is melted, remove it from the stove. In a food processor, grind the nuts and raisins. Add the chocolate, the peanut butter, the remaining one-fourth cup of milk and the hard part of the coconut milk, leaving the liquid in the can. Blend a few seconds until you get a cream, and pour over the crust. Refrigerate four hours before serving. Sprinkle some coconut flakes to decorate.

CROSTATA

This is a popular Italian dessert made with homemade jam. My favorites are fig, berries, or plum jam.

Crust:
2 cups whole wheat flour
1 Tbsp whole flaxseeds
½ Tbsp poppyseeds
½ Tbsp ground flaxseeds
¾ cup margarine
¼ cup non-dairy milk
1/8 cup raw sugar
½ lemon rind
pinch of salt

Preheat your oven at 375° F.

Filling:

It tastes better if you make your own jam, but if you are in a hurry you can use some ready-made jam. Because you will eat the dessert immediately, there is no need to put a lot of sugar with the fruit since there is no need to preserve it. Instead of one portion of fruit for half portion of sugar, I cut the sugar in half and use only raw sugar. I also add lemon zest and let it cook until the fruit holds together.

To make the crust:

In a bowl, mix the flour, salt, sugar, seeds, and lemon rind. Add the margarine by chunks, working with your hands to make it crumble. Add the milk and knead the dough until you have a ball that holds together. Cover with plastic wrap and refrigerate for half an hour. When it is ready, roll two-thirds of the dough into a circle. Put it in a round baking pan greased with margarine. Put the filling in. With the remaining dough, cut some 1/4" / 1 cm wide strips and place them over the crostata to form a crossed pattern that covers the pie. Bake for forty minutes or until golden brown. Let cool before serving so the fruit filling holds together.

CHOCOLATE LOG

This is a typical Christmas Italian dessert.

200 grams dark chocolate
150 grams vegan biscuits
3/4 cup chopped almonds
1 Tbsp agave
2 Tbsp margarine

Melt the chocolate in a bowl over a pot of hot water, adding the margarine and agave. Stir until melted.

Crush the biscuits and almonds into small pieces. Mix in the chocolate until all the biscuits and almonds are covered.

Roll a rectangular piece of foil with a piece of parchment paper on top. Pour your chocolate mixture in, forming a log. Close the parchment on it first, then the foil to shape it as a log (the parchment paper helps so the foil doesn't stick to it).

Put in the freezer for four hours, then another hour in the fridge.

Remove the parchment paper and foil gently and put it on a tray.

Decorate with powdered sugar sifted on top.

RANDOM:
BECHAMELLE (WHITE SAUCE)

This sauce is versatile and handy. You can put it on almost everything, but remember that it is quite caloric.

> 3 Tbsp margarine
> ½ cup white flour
> 34 fluid ounces (or 1 lt) non-dairy milk
> salt
> pepper
> pinch of nutmeg

On medium heat, melt the margarine in a small pot. Add the flour and mix well until it creates a soft paste. Add the milk gradually and stir well so that there are no lumps. Reduce to low heat and let cook until the sauce thickens, stirring regularly. Season with salt, pepper, and nutmeg. If you still have lumps in your sauce, blend it until smooth.

ICED COCCONUCCINO

> 1 cup coffee
> 1 can coconut cream
> ¼ cup agave
> 2 cups ice cubes
> 1 tsp vanilla extract
> 1 cup non-dairy milk

Blend all, serve cold, drink!

VEG RICOTTA

I attempted to create the easiest veg ricotta possible. I like it so much that I use it in a lot of recipes when I don't want to use a bechamelle sauce, which is heavier. It doesn't taste much as it is, but helps with the creaminess and is also a good way to impress people—homemade stuff like that is always good to convince people that eating vegan is easy!

> *34 fluid ounces (or 1 liter) soy milk*
> *5 Tbsp apple cider vinegar*

Boil the soy milk, being careful not to burn it, and add the vinegar. Let it curdle for a few seconds, remove it from the heat, and with a really fine strainer, drain the water so only the solid part remains. Use it immediately or store in the fridge for a couple of days.
You can use it to make scrambled ricotta instead of scrambled tofu.
Optional: Gently fry an onion in a pan with olive oil. Add the ricotta, turmeric, nutritional yeast, chilies, mixed herbs, salt, and pepper. It works perfectly!

KALE CHIPS

> *bunch of kale*
> *olive oil*
> *nutritional yeast flakes*
> *taco mix spices*

Remove the kale stems and cut the leaves roughly. In a bowl, mix some olive oil, nutritional yeast flakes, and taco spice mix. Mix the kale leaves in so that every leaf gets wet and becomes tender and rub them a little.
Pour on a tray, making sure to spread the leaves as much as possible.
Bake in the oven at 180° F for two hours, until crunchy.

This base can serve as a Spanish tortilla recipe starter. You just need to chop potatoes, bell pepper, and onion really small, fry them separately, pour some chickpea batter on top, and let each side cook with a lid on. It is a bit more challenging, but once you get the farinata right, try with the tortillas! I make them especially for my friend Eva, from Barcelona, who loves them. If you have a problem holding the tortilla together, add two teaspoons of cornstarch with four tablespoons of water to the batter.

Chickpea Omelette/Farinata

SOY FREE **WHEAT FREE**

This is an Italian chickpea crepe, which is done differently according to the regions of Italy. This version is easy to make and is a great savory snack or appetizer.

1 small white onion, optional
1 cup chickpea flour
1 cup water
salt
pepper
olive oil

Gently heat the chopped onion in a pan with olive oil. Meanwhile, mix the flour, salt, pepper, and water vigorously (you can put it in a blender if you want a perfect consistency, but hand mixing works). When the onion is frying, add a scoop of the mixture in the pan, just like a crepe, not thick. Cook on both sides. Cut into triangles and serve warm, don't let it cool, as it will dry out.

MORNING TOFU

WHEAT FREE

1 pack of firm tofu
vegetable oil
½ Cup soy milk plus ¾ Cup soy milk
1 teaspoon apple cider vinegar
1 lemon, juiced
¼ Cup nutritional yeast flakes
2 Tbsp Dijon mustard
1 tsp chives
1 tsp paprika
1 tsp mustard powder
salt
pepper
½ tsp Tabasco sauce, optional
1 tsp turmeric

In a blender, cover the blades with some soy milk and add a teaspoon of apple cider vinegar. Let it curdle for a few minutes, then blend for a few seconds. Continue blending on high, slowly adding some vegetable oil, until you get the consistency of a mayo sauce. Stop blending, add the other ingredients, including the rest of the soy milk, and stir into a creamy sauce.
Crush the tofu into small pieces with your hands and mix into two-thirds of the sauce. Toss well.
Serve on toasted bread.
Leftovers can be used in a salad, a sandwich, and so on.

MORNING SMOOTHIE

SOY FREE
WHEAT FREE
RAW

This is a rich smoothie, perfect to keep you going all morning until lunch without snacking, or before exercising.

¾ cup macadamia nuts
3 pitted dates
1 Tbsp goji berries
1 Tbsp flax or chia seeds
2 cup water
1 banana, 1 orange, and another fruit of your picking

Blend the macadamia nuts with the water on high speed until creamy. Add the dates and blend again. Add the rest of the ingredients, blend, and enjoy!

ACT

PART 3

There are many people that dedicate their time and energy to a cause they believe in—animal rights, conservation, human rights, feminism, and so on. I have always admired the courage of certain individuals that put their face and themselves on the front line to denounce, protest, and act against injustice. There are many ways to be an effective activist, in a spectrum from demos and petitions to direct action and intervention. My intention is to reunite all of these approaches. They are complementary and, therefore, fundamental to each other.

I want to give homage to people that, without looking for any glory, inspire me by their strength, their hope, and their courage. I want to share and spread the stories of what they do as much as possible. No one can be on all fronts and no one is expected to. Each of us can do a little, choosing to get involved in something we care for. We can improve our society, our relation towards others, and our planet.

I have interviewed people that I've met through my experience in activism, and I also want to mention a few other projects that are worth supporting. There are many more throughout the world, and this is only the tip of the iceberg!

There are many individuals and organizations around the world that are amazingly committed to defending those who cannot defend themselves.

Animal Liberation Victoria—**ALV** is an abolitionist organization dedicated to helping all animals, with a strong focus on those who are factory farmed. The underlying goal of ALV is to abolish the property status of animals. ALV is located in Melbourne and acknowledged and respected as Victoria's most premier vegan abolitionist animal rights organization.   www.alv.org.au

Coalition for the protection of racehorses—The racing industry has operated for over 150 years without giving much consideration to the animals they exploit. As a result, CPR was formed in 2008 in Australia to address the animal welfare concerns that are rife throughout the racing industry. By using public opinion and concern, CPR is able to address these serious animal welfare concerns and bring positive changes for the animals and the industry.

www.horseracingkills.com

Committee Against the Bird Slaughter—The CABS is an action operational society that intervenes when bird trappers, hunters, or animal traders commit offenses against current nature protection legislation in Europe. In addition, through initiatives at parliamentary level, they attempt improvements in the legal guidelines for wildlife, nature, and species protection. The CABS execute well-organized operations in many European states where migrant birds are illegally persecuted by the use of traps, nets, line, sticks, or are shot. The CABS operate hand-in-hand with local conservationists and the police. They collect more than 50,000 mist nets and traps annually, monitor hundreds of hunters, and support the police in bringing poachers to justice.

http://www.komitee.de/en

Edgar's Mission—Edgar's Mission is a nonprofit farm sanctuary that seeks to create a humane and just world for humans and non-humans, situated a couple of hours north of Melbourne, Australia.

http://www.edgarsmission.org.au

Elephant Nature Park—In northern Thailand, near Chiang Mai, is a sanctuary for elephants and many other animals (dogs, monkeys, and many more) that is home for distressed animals rescued from all over Thailand. Some of the elephants were used as slaves for tree logging, others suffered mine bombing, and some were used as an attraction fr tourists in the city. A vegetarian restaurant in Chang Mai, *Taste From Heaven*, helps to raise funds for the sanctuary.

http://www.elephantnaturepark.org

International Anti-Poaching Foundation—The illegal trafficking of wildlife now ranks as the 3rd largest criminal industry in the world. IAPF warriors effectively fight poaching and safeguard elephants, rhinos and other endangered wildlife.

www.iapf.org

Projeto Mucky—Projeto Mucky shares the idea that all living creatures are entitled to life, care, and respect. Founded in 1985, its objective is to assist and care for primates found in physically or emotionally poor condition because of bad treatment or abandonment. Focusing on the steady consideration of life as a universal gift granted to all beings, the project develops its activities in its own site in Itu (San Paolo, Brazil) and presently shelters several species of Brazilian primates, performing medic/veterinary assistance, offering them shelter and non-stop care. The project develops important educational work to raise society's awareness regarding primates' condition as wild animals (therefore they should live in the wild), and is committed to the fight against animal traffic.

www.projetomucky.org

Soi Dog Foundation—Soi Dog is a nonprofit organization that helps the homeless, neglected, and abused cats and dogs of Thailand, through medical care, sterilization, and care. They set an example for the Asian region on how to humanely reduce the number of unwanted dogs and cats through spaying and neutering, and to better the lives and living conditions of the stray dogs and feral cats of Asia.

www.soidog.org

Surfers for Cetaceans—S4C activates ocean-minded people everywhere to support the conservation and protection of whales, dolphins, and marine life. Through compassion, awareness, education, media, and dedicated interventions they seek to be a human voice for and defender of cetaceans worldwide.   http://www.s4cglobal.org

Women for Whales—WfW creates and supports a universal collaboration for the protection and conservation of all conscious, breathing, marine mammals through pro-active, positive, and peaceful methods. They plan to hold an International Whale Celebration outside each International Whaling Commission (IWC) meeting. The International Whale Celebration was created in 2011 to raise awareness of the IWC meeting and peacefully protest the killing and capture of cetaceans. Whales should be celebrated and WfW will continue to peacefully stand up for them until the International Whaling Commission truly conserves and protects whales and dolphins across the world.

www.womenforwhales.org
www.facebook.com/celebratewhales

SEA SHEPHERD CONSERVATION SOCIETY

I have been involved with Sea Shepherd since 2010, when the organization gave me the opportunity to become a better activist—and a better cook.

Sea Shepherd was founded in 1977 by Paul Watson as a "...non-profit conservation organization whose mission was to end the destruction of habitat and slaughter of wildlife in the world's oceans in order to conserve and protect ecosystems and species." Sea Shepherd uses non-violent direct action to intervene in cases of illegal poaching, overfishing, marine pollution, and situations that put the eco-system of our oceans in danger. Sea Shepherd acts on behalf of the law, like the World Charter for Nature of 1982 that states that nature conservation is a universal principle and obligation of all and it is the duty of all to protect it. Sea Shepherd targets criminals that are violating international laws.

In 1977, Watson bought his first boat, the Sea Shepherd, in order to stop a pirate whaling boat, the Sierra. And as Paul always says, "What better than pirates to stop pirates? We are pirates of compassion, hunting down and destroying pirates of profit." What you need is direct action, intervention, activism, not bureaucracy and words if you really want to make a difference and stop the slaughter that is happening in our oceans. Not only did the Sierra cease their illegal activity, but in the next two years, three more whaling boats did, too. Focusing on the source of the problem is the key to efficient combating of illegal activities. This has been the line that Sea Shepherd has followed over the last 37 years, becoming one of the most effective organizations in defense of marine wild life.

People often ask, "why the oceans and not other issues?" Sea Shepherd has maintained its integrity and efficiency in direct action activism because it has focused on one aspect of the fight for the environment and the Earth. Focusing on the oceans doesn't mean not caring about other issues. Many people on board the Sea Shepherd ships are activists elsewhere as well, and there is constant interaction with people that fight to save the forests, aboriginal and indigenous lands, factory farm animals, and human rights around the globe. Watson is also the founder of organizations Earthforce and Friends of the Wolf. Choosing to dedicate much of your energy to one issue is not giving up on other issues. However, with many struggles needed for our planet, a person cannot always be effective if they are

spread too thin.

The oceans cover 70% of our planet and are in a critical state due to the over-exploitation of resources. It doesn't take much to realize that, to quote Paul, "If the oceans die, we die." Oceans are a source of oxygen for humans. It is psychotic behavior to destroy what is keeping us alive. This is why we fight and take back what is the property of no one except planet Earth. It is ridiculous to live in a world where water is sold in bottles, when there is water all around us. It is ridiculous to ignore the three laws of biodiversity: diversity of the species, interdependence of the species, and limited resources. Those three aspects explain why we have to save the marine species of our oceans, from krill to whales, if we want to survive on this planet.

The most famous Sea Shepherd campaign is the anti-whaling campaign in Antarctica, but Sea Shepherd is or has been active on many other fronts: Blue Fin tuna in the Mediterranean, sharks in the Pacific, dolphins in Taiji, pilot whales in the Faroe Islands, seals in Canada and Namibia, whales in the North Atlantic and Pacific, and many more. Sea Shepherd's philosophy is best summed up as: "Intelligence is the ability of a species to live in harmony with its environment." Whether we learn to respect and protect our surrounding, it is up to us, but the action of many passionate individuals is our only way to survive on this planet.

Peter Hammarstedt's
PEANUT SATAY STIR-FRY

Peter has been a longtime Sea Shepherd and the captain of the Bob Barker since operation Divine Wind. I crewed with him during that campaign and this is one of his favorite meals, together with raw smoothies and noodles.

RICH PEANUT SATAY SAUCE

1 lime juice

1 garlic clove

3 Tbsp soy sauce

6 Tbsp peanut butter (smooth and sugar-free)

½ can coconut cream (200 ml)

½ tsp raw sugar

½ tsp fresh ginger

chili flakes, optional

2 tsp rice vinegar or white vinegar

Blend all ingredients until creamy. Use the sauce as a dip for spring rolls (page 40-41) or for your favorite veggie stir-fry.

There are a million ways to make a good stir-fry. I heat a little bit of coconut oil with minced shallot, ginger, garlic, and chili flakes. Add some chopped bell peppers, broccoli, and mushrooms. Season with Braggs or tamari and cook about ten minutes so the vegetables are still crunchy. At the end, add your favorite green leaf (bok choy, kale, spinach) and cook another few minutes.

Serve with rice and peanut sauce.

GREAT BEAR FOREST- INTERVIEW WITH TOMMY KNOWLES

What is the Great Bear Forest, what species live there, and what issues are they facing?

The Great Bear Rainforest is on the West Coast of Northern British Columbia, Canada. It is the largest, intact, temperate rainforest on the planet and features 1000-year-old Western Red Cedar and 90-meter Sitka Spruce.

The area is home to grizzly bears, black bears, wolves, cougars, orca whales, humpback whales, among other species. Most notably though, is the Kermode or, "Spirit Bear."

There is a particular species of Black Bear that carry a really rare gene. Can you describe it?

One thing that makes the Great Bear Rainforest so special is that black bears within the forest carry a rare gene that makes one in ten cubs white. The Kermode or, "Spirit Bear," traverses the Great Bear Rainforest and is protected under law from hunting of any kind.

There is trophy hunting allowed in the forest. Who issues the licence and what are the hunters allowed to kill?

Each year, the British Columbian government issues licenses to hunters who want to trophy hunt within the Great Bear Rainforest. The trophy hunters focus on killing grizzly bears, black bears, wolves, and cougars.

What is the idea of the campaign that you are working on to stop trophy hunting? What tactics can you use to be efficient?

In 2012, while sailing to Antarctica to defend whales from the illegal slaughter conducted by the Japanese government, I formed the Wildlife Defense League. The League was formed in order to raise awareness about conservation issues facing Canada and to directly intervene when conservation laws were being broken. We are still in the early stages of developing the organization but have an experienced group of people willing to take on the task.

Our first campaign, Operation Great Bear, will focus on the trophy hunt in the Great Bear Rainforest. Trophy hunters kill roughly 360 grizzly bears each year. To the trophy hunters, these iconic animals mean nothing more than a rug on the wall and a good story to tell.

The Wildlife Defense League will protect the grizzly bear, black bear, and the wolf in the Great Bear Rainforest from the annual, senseless slaughter known as the British Columbia Trophy Hunt. We will expose, document, and intervene when necessary against hunters and poachers, all while abiding by international conservation law and law set out by First Nations of Canada.

Is there support from the local population, and more specifically, from the First Nations, that have been stewards of land more than anyone else?

Last year, First Nations put an outright ban on trophy hunting within the Great Bear Rainforest but the government and the hunters do not respect this ban. The Wildlife Defense League is currently working with conservation organizations and First Nations to develop a strategy that will stop trophy hunters.

Is there a legal background which you can refer to, in order to intervene?

The Wildlife Defense League's primary mandate is to assume a law enforcement role as provided by the United Nations World Charter for Nature and an enforcement role to uphold laws set by First Nations of Canada.

A general principle laid out by the Charter states that the genetic viability on the Earth shall not be compromised; the population levels of all life forms, wild and domesticated, must be sufficient for their survival, and to this, necessary habitats shall be safeguarded.

We work to ensure that habitat is safeguarded.

Do you believe in direct action as a way to intervene against animals and environment destruction?

I strongly believe that direct action is the best way to intervene against the onslaught of animals and Earth. No government has ever acted until direct action by individuals was taken. If we wait on government to enact laws to protect animals and the environment, we will be too late. I believe that we should never compromise in defense of Mother Earth.

158 · THINK EAT ACT

What about the Northern Gateway Pipelines— are there collaborations between the two campaigns?

The Wildlife Defense League is not collaborating the trophy hunt campaign with the Northern Gateway Pipeline campaign but we hold the position that the Northern Gateway Pipeline must not go through. We stand in solidarity with those who oppose Enbridge and this destructive project.

Conservation groups like Pacific Wild are tackling both issues and I suggest anyone interested in anything to do with the Great Bear Rainforest to visit www.pacificwild.org. They have spearheaded the conservation movement and originally inspired me to get involved in conservation.

How do you fund your campaign and how can people support it?

Our campaigns are funded by private donations from individuals and groups concerned with protecting wild nature.

If you would like to help support the Wildlife Defense League, please visit and like our Facebook page, Wildlife Defense League or visit www.wildlifedefenseleague.wordpress.com and click on the donate button.

We appreciate any support!

Like many other activists, you are vegan. Is there any recipe you would like to submit? What is your favorite recipe?

I suggest eating anything within this cookbook. Raffa taught me so much about veganism and was an amazing support system. I credit her with helping me make a compassionate step to a better life. She is, by far, the best chef I know! If I had to pick something within the cookbook, I'd say try her cookies. They are insanely good and keep me going on long days in Antarctica.

VANCOUVER ANIMAL DÉFENSE LEAGUE-
INTERVIEW WITH MARLEY DAVIDUK

Can you describe Vancouver Animal Defense League and its aim?

The Vancouver Animal Defense League is a small grassroots animal rights organization that focuses on sustained protest campaigns targeting companies and individuals who profit off of animal abuse and exploitation.

One of your main campaigns at the moment is to ban shark fin in British Columbia and Canada. Can you talk about this campaign?

This is the first time I worked on a legislation campaign and I started it without expectations and little faith in my government. Canada has one of the worst reputations in the world for environmental destruction and total disregard for wildlife, and I thought it would be almost impossible to get them to risk trade disruption by banning this symbolic Chinese product. But sharks are facing extinction and I felt like I needed to do everything I could to stop it, even if it means working on a legislative campaign with a small chance of success. We started presenting to city councils, requesting that they ban shark fin because three cities had done that on their own. I had partnered with local Chinese-Canadian activist Anthony Marr and we presented to local city councils and in six months we were able to convince seven cities to ban the sale of shark fins. We needed more than municipal bans but we thought this would get the ball rolling for a Federal or Provincial ban.

On March 27th, the federal government voted on a shark fin ban. We had worked for a year to gain support for this bill and we had enough Members of Parliament to vote in favor and win, but Stephen Harper "whipped" the vote—he told his Conservative Party members to block it regardless of what they wanted to do. We were told by several conservative MP's that even though they wanted to support the bill, they were facing "external pressure" to vote otherwise. We lost by five votes and I don't know if any other organization in Canada that has been that close to changing legislation to protect wildlife. What could I expect from a federal government responsible for the Canadian seal slaughter? We are now focusing on a provincial campaign to ban the sale and trade of shark fins in BC and there is a lot more hope.

One of the most important things we have done is DNA testing on shark fins for sale here in BC. We partnered with CTV news station and went to Chinese apothecaries to purchase $2,000 worth of fins. We had them DNA tested at a laboratory at Guelph University and the results were shocking. 86% of what we tested was endangered, threatened, or vulnerable as defined by the International Union for the Conservation of Nature, but none of them were banned species. Since we have done these tests, the Convention on the International Trade of Endangered Species have added five more shark species to the protected list and three of those we found for sale here (Porbeagle, Scalloped Hammerhead, and Great Hammerhead). We plan on DNA testing again once the CITES ban finalizes in 2014 and if we find the same species, we can shut down the importers and hopefully the Federal government will be forced to reconsider a ban, otherwise they would be in violation of international law for allowing the sale of an endangered species.

There is a lot of political lobbying with emails and pressure for politicians, but also a lot of direct action with protest in front of restaurants that sell shark fin soup. How do you combine the two aspects and would you say that they are complementary?

I think we are the only group in Canada who chooses to take part in shark fin legislation campaigns and protest campaigns at the same time and we do that simply because I refuse to spend years of my life begging the government to do something with the risk of nothing happening in the end. If the Federal, Provincial, and Municipal governments all fail to take action at least we have been targeting the restaurants and the sale of shark fins. We started by protesting at Fortune Garden Seafood restaurant and after eight months they agreed to take it off the menu because our demonstrations nearly destroyed their business. On the days we were protesting, the restaurant was almost empty. We sent the majority of their customers to other restaurants and I think they were coming close to financial ruin. We have since moved on to Sun Sui Wah, which is a much larger restaurant, but we are doing the same, systematically tearing apart their business by ruining dinner service with our loud, energetic demos and sending their customers away.

Many people are happy to join the boycott once they find out that this restaurant sells as much or more shark fins than any other restaurant in the city. I think that protest campaigns are one of the most effective ways to target the sale of cruel products like shark fins, fur, or foie gras as long as they are sustained campaigns with increasing pressure over time.

What are the risks involved in doing these direct action protests? I assume it is legal in BC to protest in a public space, but are there loopholes used to try to make you stop?

We generally have to deal with police when protesting, often, the restaurant will call the police but they cannot do anything as long as we are not breaking the law. We have to make sure our activists are not trespassing or blocking the entrance of the restaurant and then we should have nothing to worry about.

What is the general feeling of the population in Canada about shark fin?

I have been protesting for fourteen years and I have never received as much support from the public as I have with the shark fin demos. With fur or foie gras, people will abuse you, call you names, throw stuff at you and shame you, but with shark fins the general attitude is much more positive. Sometimes the honks from cars passing the demo are so loud that we can't hear each other, there will be half a dozen cars honking and waving at a time. There is so much love and support for sharks thanks to the documentary *Sharkwater* and all of the media surrounding the campaign, everyone seems to know about this issue and understand its importance. The problem is we have more shark fins for sale in Canada than almost anywhere in the world, other than China itself. This means there are a lot of people financially invested in it who are willing to fight tooth and nail against a ban.

Some restaurants actually have banned shark fin soup thanks to your protest. Do you go further and try to explain that many more of the animals they are serving are also risking extinction or do you prefer to go one step at the time and focus first on sharks?

When targeting the restaurants, we only approach them with the shark fin issue, but when educating the public, we use vegan literature. I find it is very easy for people here to criticize a Chinese dish like shark fin while totally disregarding the inhumane treatment of farm animals in Canada which I think needs to be addressed. I think that the issue of shark fins is a great way to get the general public involved in an animal rights/ environmental issue where discussions can begin about the treatment of all animals in the food system, allowing them to reflect on cruel traditions they may be taking part in. When people point out how cruel it is that sharks have their fins cut off while fully conscious, I am sure to let them know that farm animals have their beaks seared off, tails snipped, and ears clipped all while fully conscious as well.

Do you do other campaigns aside shark fin bans?

We primarily focus on fur, sharks, rodeo, vegan outreach, and vivisection. We have an ongoing fur campaign against Winners, a Canadian clothing store and we protest them all winter. Winners, has more than 200 stores across Canada and they stopped selling fur in seven of them because of our efforts. We try not to take too much on because it dilutes our efforts if we are targeting too many issues at once.

Do you get support from local people or from other animal/environmental organizations?

We have a core group of activists who regularly take part in our demos. There are not a lot of us, but we are effective. We don't need massive amounts of people to get a business to change their ways, we just need some people who are willing to dedicate their time to protesting. We do not back down until we get what we want, even if it takes years. When I started VADL five years ago. Our first campaign was against Snowflake Furs. We wanted them evicted out of the Fairmont Hotel Vancouver and it took two years of consistent protests but we won and they were kicked out and we did that with only a handful of people.

How can people support Vancouver Animal Defense League?

People can donate at vancouveranimaldefenseleague.blogspot.com
        We are fundraising to buy a professional projector so we can do vegan outreach with a mobile movie screen. With a portable projector, we can set up a white screen or even project on the side of a building. With speakers and sound, people will have a hard time walking past our leaflets without seeing the painful reality countless animals are facing.

FRUIT COCKTAIL CAKE

This was my mother's recipe and it was a perfect cake for being at sea when you are out of fresh fruit, the cupboards are bare, and all you have left is canned fruit!

1 1/2 cups sugar
2 cups flour
2 tsp baking soda
1/2 tsp salt
Egg replacer equal to 2 eggs
14 oz of tinned fruit
(fruit cocktail, peaches, pears, or crushed pineapple)

Add all ingredients except for flour and blend, then add flour.
Bake in a 9 x 3 greased pan and bake at 350° for fourty-five minutes.

Icing

3/4 cup of sugar
1/2 cup soy cream
1/2 cup margarine
1 tsp vanilla

Boil all ingredients except vanilla.
Add vanilla, pour over the hot cake, and serve warm!

SHARK DEFENSE AUSTRALIA- INTERVIEW WITH JORDAN CROOKE

In April 2012, I started Australia's first "Fin Free" group "Fin Free Ranges" with the aim of ridding the Yarra Ranges of the ecologically destructive delicacy of shark fin soup, a dish that is contributing to the decimation of shark populations world-wide and encouraging the poaching of shark body parts.

Our small group helped pass the first motion by any level of government in Australia against shark finning and shark products. In August 2012, the Shire of Yarra Ranges unanimously voted to pass a motion condemning the practice of shark finning. They agreed to write letters to restaurants serving shark fin soup to ask them to go 'fin-free' while banning the consumption of shark fin soup and all shark products at council events.

As I came to learn more about sharks and the many threats they face, I decided we needed more then a "Fin Free" group. So I decided to start Shark Defense Australia with a few mates of mine to take on the many threats facing sharks in Australia like culling in W.A, N.S.W and Queensland, poaching, habitat destruction, pollution, and the trading of endangered species. The motto of Shark Defense Australia is Science-Education-Action.

We aim to work with scientists to get strong scientific data to educate the general public to get real, long-term action for sharks.

We are running a few campaigns, including campaigns to get Ebay to stop the sale of shark products, helping to start a new "Fin Free" group in local communities, breaking the shark fin trade in Australia, and helping take down the shark culling nets on the East coast of Australia.

Sharks have existed for over 400 million years, have survived six major extinctions, and are apex predators. They regulate the ocean ecosystems, which produce 70% of the oxygen we breathe. Despite their integral role in keeping us alive, sharks are at threat of being wiped out completely within our lifetime. All of this as a result of human greed and ignorance. Even if we can't get you to love sharks as much as we do, I hope we can get you to respect both them and their importance to the health of our planet. We must take action now for sharks. "There can be them without us, but there can be no us without them" #LoveSharks

Can you talk about sharks in their ecosystem and how important they are to the oceans? Can we already see consequences and changes in our oceans due to the slaughter of sharks?

Sharks are an apex predator, which means that they are at the top of the marine food chain, along with other fishes like tuna and marlin. They have the whole ecosystem under them. If they disappear, all of the smaller species underneath them, like rays, small, or medium fishes, will explode. There will come a point where they will not have enough to eat because the food chain's balance has been broken. Around Japan, we have an explosion of jellyfish because of shark extinction. Scientists still have to do a lot of studies because we don't know the absolute consequences yet, but it can't be good when a species is destined to be eradicated. To understand the importance of apex predators, the case of Yellowstone is perfect. All the wolves were hunted, so the forest diminished because the deer population exploded—they were eating the saplings (baby trees). As a result, trees stopped growing and the grass expanded. It took awhile to realize the crucial role of wolves and their reintroduction in the park has re-balanced the ecosystem.

There is a misperception of sharks with people fearing them more than how actually dangerous they are. How do you fight that?

With Shark Defense Australia, we act as a "PR" group for sharks. We react to bad news coverage and talk for the sharks. We say what the reality is; that sharks are not the main danger for human beings, but there is a paranoia around them based on propaganda.

We repeat advice to avoid shark attacks, like not to swim at dusk or dawn when they feed, don't swim in a seal colony; common sense, really.

It is important to know that only six species of sharks out of 400 have attacked people, while we tend to talk about sharks as a single entity not distinguished.

Studies have shown that attacks only occur when water temperature is above 70° F / 21° C, so the rising water temperature, due to global warming, can attract shark populations that were not there originally.

Sharks do not attack us to eat us. They attack us by mistake or out of fear, but they actually do not get any nutrients from us, so it's important to be realistic.

What can you do to be effective in shark fin ban campaigns? Can you describe more about the Ebay campaign, for example? What other campaigns to you plan to do?

We are pushing for a full ban for the import and export in Australia concerning all shark products (fins, jaws, teeth, liver oil, cartilage…). We are engaged in a study with the university of Tasmania to test shark fins to see where they come from, and so far they have all come from Indonesia, Hong Kong, India, and China, which have "unsustainable fisheries," not regulated and more likely to do finning—a practice that deprives the shark from its fin. They throw the body overboard to an agonizing, slow, and horrible death, all for the consumption of shark fin soup, a dish popular in a lot of Asian countries. This is a first step to push the Australian government to take quick action on the "sustainable" argument.

In 2012, Australia exported 178 tons of fins, and more and more scientists find that the fin fisheries in Queensland and Northern territories are unsustainable too, where the sharks are thrown overboard, because of loopholes in the legislation that ban the poaching of sharks.

We do these studies for public awareness and to push politicians to change the laws.

We have four official campaigns at the moment:
· Fin testing to see where they come from
· Helping people to start fin free groups, with logistic, logos, and any other sort of help, to have more and more local active groups
· Propose to make the great barrier reef a shark sanctuary like in Palau or American Samoa. Sharks are worth a million more alive than dead, for tourism but also to save a beautiful, but fragile ecosystem
· The Ebay campaign to stop the trade and trafficking of shark products through their website. We mobilize the local communities to report endangered sharks pieces that are for sale so Ebay can remove them from their list. We need Ebay to go further, to ban the sell of any shark products that encourage poaching.

Do you think direct action is one of the ways of stopping shark finning?

Our motto says "science, education, and action". If we were to be in a situation of illegal poaching, we would act. We take example from Sea Shepherd and the International aAnti-Poaching Foundation, an NGO based in Africa and Australia, which protects wildlife, with more information at www.iapf.org/en/about

Specializing in sharks makes us more likely to focus all our energy on one problem, and we do believe in direct action as part of the solution to protect endangered lives.

Do you have hope that things can change and that shark populations can grow back to what they were before human intervention?

I have a lot of hope. We need to give time to Mother Nature, and whether we start to work together or not, she is gonna chew us up and spit us out!

www.sharkdefenseaustralia.org.au

Jordan suggests that you look up online a vegan recipe for shark fin soup, a cruelty free version of the infamous traditional soup that costs the lives of millions of sharks each year.

THE HUNT SABOTEURS ASSOCIATION- INTERVIEW WITH ADAM

The Hunt Saboteurs Association was formed in Winter of 1963 and went into action on Boxing day in South Devon, England. From that day, Hunt Saboteurs have taken action against organized bloodsports all over the country. Hunt Saboteurs (sabs) mainly concentrate on, but are not limited to, organized Fox hunts, Stag hunts, Mink Hunts, Beagle and Basset Packs, and Shoots.

Currently we have over 30 groups across the UK, each comprised of about eight people. All active and attending hunts at least once per week. New groups across other parts of Europe are also forming and becoming active.

We have a committee of up to thirteen members comprised of active sabs who perform the various roles (merchandise, admin, press, etc.) which help attract donations that go straight to local groups. Each of these committee members are elected and face re-election every year. Every group remains autonomous and print their own literature and merchandise, as well as give interviews on behalf of the movement without anyone's permission. Through this structure, we remain a resilient grass-roots movement of decentralized, autonomous groups who have an elected committee to act as a representative for the groups in the media, but without this committee the movement would continue regardless and hunts would continue to be sabotaged. The main challenge of our structure is in fund raising and interactions with the media. This is improving as time goes on, but perhaps with a different structure like having a representative, we'd attract more media contacts and donations, but we can only speculate.

Our campaigns are funded mostly by ourselves, with the main costs of fuel, equipment and vehicle maintenance falling on individual groups and usually on the sabs themselves to fund their activities out of their own pocket. Groups raise funds in any way they can, usually by benefit gigs, etc. which help for some of the costs, and recently we've had support from the cosmetic company Lush whose help has lead to several new groups forming over the past four years. The committee runs a website and social media sites through which the public can buy merchandise and memberships which provide funds which go to groups.

All our campaigns involve direct action, mostly against the various bloodsports which take place in the UK, and more recently against a cull of Badgers proposed by the current government. The techniques we employ to sabotage these bloodsports vary. For Fox and Hare hunting, we typically adopt techniques the hunts use to encourage their hounds to chase and kill, to encourage them away from their quarry. Often this involves the use of hunting horns and voice calls, which the hounds are trained to respond to, and techniques we've developed, such as citronella spray to mask the scent of the fox. Most recently, audio devices to play the sound of excited hounds "on cry", which their pack mentality urges them to follow. Since fox and hare hunting were banned in 2004 under the hunting act, hunts are increasingly put off by cameras, which lead every year to convictions for illegal hunting, prompting the rise of members of the public taking to "hunt monitoring" rather than sabbing and has provided some excellent footage over the years. Since the bloodsports we campaign against tend to take place on private land, we have to sabotage on private land. Traditionally, this was a civil offense rather than a criminal offense, meaning that police powers could not be used to remove us. But the Criminal Justice and Public Order Act 1994 introduced a new Offense of Aggravated Trespass, which made it a criminal offense to trespass with the intention to "interfere with a legal pursuit," and gave the police a new power to use against hunt sabotage. Although many arrests have been made under the offense, few convictions come from it. However, it was a convenient tool in the huntsman's arsenal against saboteurs- that was until the hunting act came into force, making the pursuits we interfere in no longer legal. It's still used to arrest saboteurs or move us off private land, but it is not used as much as it used to be.

For transport, we typically use old Land Rover Defender vehicles, which can seat up to eight or nine sabs at a time, and drive around the various country lanes and fields we may need to traverse. Typically, a driver and a navigator remain in the vehicle while sabs enter fields on foot. The driver and the navigator's jobs are often impeded by hunt supporters blocking roads and quite commonly attacking the vehicle, sometimes attacking the driver and the navigator.

Traditionally the movement is 50/50 men to women, with women playing just as much of a crucial role as men. The reaction of hunt supporters to women can vary, but most often they have no issue with hitting, pushing, or riding their horses over women as they do to men. We do suspect that they see women as being physically inferior, as they tend to be more aggressive to the males in groups that are mostly female. They see the males as being outnumbered, despite the presence of the female sabs. It's usually to their surprise that the female sabs are more than capable of standing up for themselves in the face of violence.

Local support depends on the area. Some sab groups operate in heavily pro-hunt areas and wear masks when they are out sabbing to avoid revenge attacks against their homes or families. While other sab groups have no problem holding stalls, organizing benefit gigs, or other types of fundraisers. In general, the majority of paying HSA members are from the countryside but are unable to voice their opposition to the local hunt for fear of reprisal from their bullying supporters. That's where the HSA come in.

The vast majority of sabs are vegan. From the outset, most sabs were vegetarian out of general respect for animals but as more information was gathered on hunting, the role that hunts play within agriculture became apparent. To their local area, hunts provide a service of collecting and disposing of lame or dead animals, which they skin and feed to their hounds. The animals can be anything, but tend to be horses, sheep, pigs, or dairy calves. The majority of animals are dairy calves, the male calves of dairy cows bred for their milk, but useless because of their gender. So once there's an animal that is of no commercial value, the local hunt comes around with a hand gun, shoots it, and takes it away in their "carcass wagon" for their hounds. To use animal products is to breed animals, and to breed animals is to produce a surplus of animals which will eventually be disposed of, thereby producing the perfect reason for a hunt to exist. Go vegan.

SUPPORT VEGAN PRISONERS-
INTERVIEW WITH JAKE CONROY AND ERIC MACDAVID

Jake Conroy was involved in the Shac campaign against the animal testing lab, Huntingdon Life Sciences. Jake was sentenced to four years in jail and was released to a halfway house in November 2009, and is recently released from federal probation.

Can you talk about the Shac campaign, especially in the U.S.?

Stop Huntingdon Animal Cruelty USA (SHAC USA) helped coordinate the international movement to close the notorious animal-testing laboratory, Huntingdon Life Sciences (HLS). HLS is a contract research organization based in England and the USA that tests other companies' products on just about any animal, from mice and rats, to dogs, cats, and wild-caught baboons. They kill 500 animals each day to test products "safe" for human use, such as oven cleaners, food coloring, and crap pharmaceuticals like Viagra.

SHAC USA spearheaded the campaign in the U.S. by doing research on protest targets and the laboratory, devising, and implementing strategies, organizing local and national demonstrations, publishing leaflets, posters, videos, and newsletters, and maintaining a webpage that kept people up to date on the campaign and provided a space for activists from around the world to publicize their actions, regardless of what they were.

The anti-HLS campaign galvanized the grassroots movement and reminded them that we didn't need big organizations, large salaries (or any salaries, for that matter), or endless access to resources to be successful. We needed creativity, dedication, and the knowledge that we could do it ourselves. Victories would be hard-fought, but as we toppled the largest financial and pharmaceutical corporations in the world, we realized the beauty in our power. We recognized that there wasn't just one way to get the job done, rather a whole toolbox of tactics that should be embraced, or at the very least, understood. We were reminded that our solidarity and passion was stronger than their money and influence and it terrified them—because we were winning.

Under what law did you get arrested and tried? What were your charges and how long did you stay in prison for?

Ultimately, the U.S. government, at the request of the industries, cracked down on us, and six of us wound up in U.S. federal court, indicted on multiple felonies. They singled out Lauren Gazzola, Kevin Kjonaas, and myself as the so-called "ringleaders" and charged us, tried us, and found us guilty of a variety of conspiracy charges. They weren't saying we engaged in any of the illegal activities that happened during the campaign, but because we operated a webpage that publicized those activities after they occurred, because we supported the ideologies of those tactics, and simply shared those ideas, we were just as guilty as those who actually broke the law.

We were found guilty of conspiring to violate the 1934 Telecommunications Harrasment Act (which makes it a felony to make a prank phone call across state lines), conspiracy to commit interstate stalking, and three counts of interstate stalking (because our webpage crossed state lines through the internet and encouraged people to protest against upper management of corporations, this was constituted as stalking them), and one count of conspiracy to violate the Animal Enterprise Protection Act (which all six of us and the organization were found guilty of). This is a highly controversial law in the United States, which is now called the Animal Enterprise Terrorism Act. Essentially, it states that if you cross state lines to disrupt a business that uses animals, and inflict more than $10,000 worth of damage, you can be found guilty of domestic terrorism. They claimed we conspired to cross state lines through the internet, with our web page, and caused $1,000,001 worth of economic damage to HLS.

After a lengthy trial, we were all found guilty and I was sentenced to 48 months in federal prison. I served 25 months at a medium security prison in southern California in the Mojave Desert, eleven months at a low security prison on an island in Los Angeles Harbor in Southern California, six months in a federal halfway house in Oakland, California, and am currently finishing up three years of federal probation.

What is the status of a so-called "eco-terrorist" in prison? Do you get a special treatment, such as more severe conditions?

I was labeled a domestic terrorist by the Bureau of Prisons (BOP) upon entering prison. The way you are treated because of this is decided upon by each prison. While I was incarcerated, all of my incoming and outgoing mail was opened, read, and photocopied, if need be. All of my phone calls were recorded and monitored. My visits were primarily limited to my immediate family with a couple of exceptions, for the first two years.

I was in two prisons, and the first one I was in for 25 months. It was a pretty hectic place, much like you see in the movies—full of fights, stabbings, riots, gangs, and racial politics. I was in with high-level gang members, bank robbers, rapists, and murderers. Out of 1,300 of us, I was labeled one of the top ten security threats at the institution. I had to carry a special identification card and report to a guard every two hours starting at 6:30am until 8:30pm to let them know my whereabouts, and that I hadn't escaped. If I missed a check in I faced being thrown in the segregated housing unit (SHU), otherwise known as the "hole."

Under the American law, you do not have a special right as a vegan to have a special diet. Is that the only special diet that is not allowed to prisoners?

Special diets are seen as personal preferences and are not accommodated. The only way you can get a special diet is if it falls under a religious guideline or a medical condition, and usually those are only won through legal challenges. Special diets cost the Bureau of Prisons (BOP) money, and the only way it will change is if the cost to fight against the special diet exceeds the actual cost of providing said diet.

What about allergies or intolerance? Could you say, for example, that you are intolerant to dairies to avoid them or do you get a medical check for those things?

The BOP could care less about you, your allergies, or your special diet, for that matter. They see it as a "personal preference." They will not make exceptions unless under the threat of litigation or serious repercussions. They have made a few dietary changes for Muslims and Jews, but those meals are usually not vegan. They also provide special meals for diabetics, which also are not vegan.

The one way around all of this, which is a long shot but worked for me, is to convince the medical department to prescribe you vegetables. I was lucky in that I found a BOP physician's assistant who was a Seventh Day Adventist and understood veganism. He ended up writing me a prescription for vegetables and fruit. I was one of two people out of 1,300 inmates that had the privilege to not only legally get vegetables and fruit, but also to take them back to the units to prepare them. It drove the prison crazy. While this didn't last my entire incarceration, it was an incredible perk.

What is the daily menu in prison and what time do you eat?

Meals were generally served around 7am, 11:30am, and 5pm and followed a national menu that a majority of the BOP facilities follow. It's a six-week calendar that you rotate through. The meals are required to meet a certain amount of calories per day, and have a no-meat option (95% of these options are not vegan). While the menu looks pretty good on paper, the reality is that they try and spend less than a $1.50 a day per person to feed them. The meals are high in starch and grease and contain almost no fresh vegetables or fruit. A lot of the food comes in boxes marked "NOT FIT FOR HUMAN CONSUMPTION," or come from wholesalers that need to get rid of it in a hurry because it's expired.

Can you buy vegan food from the prison commissary?

You can often find items on commissary (store) that are vegan, but that doesn't translate into good or healthy. It's a constant rotation, depending on what each prison decides to order and sell, and the selection varies depending on where you are incarcerated. In my experience, there were a number of "accidentally" vegan items— like some of the cookies and cereals and granola. What little produce they sold, like onions and jalapenos, were eventually replaced with onion powder and pickled jalapeno slices in a jar. I mainly survived off of the flour tortillas and dehydrated beans, and I relied on the black market to provide me with fresh produce, tofu, and textured vegetable protein.

Can anyone bring you food on special occasions like your birthday?

Unfortunately not. In federal prison, you are not allowed to receive anything in the mail from someone besides letters, photos, books, and magazines. There are vending machines in the visiting rooms where your visitors can purchase you food to eat during a visit, but nothing can be mailed in.

What are the ways to obtain vegan food? Can you do exchanges with other prisoners?

The black market was one of the most fascinating parts of prison life. Everything you can think of is bought and sold in prison, including vegan food. The currency in prison is postage stamps. Twenty stamps, otherwise called a "book," is worth $5 on the black market. In order to get stamps, you can either buy them at the commissary (where you're paying over $7 per book), buy them off of an inmate who is selling them (for $5 a book), or you have a hustle where you earn stamps for your services. You can use stamps to purchase items or services off of the black market, ranging from black tar heroin down to an onion smuggled out of the kitchen.

I wanted to keep the money on my account to a minimum as to avoid having to pay excessive amounts of money towards my restitution. But in order to remain vegan in prison, you need to have money to spend. So I came up with a couple of hustles to earn stamps. I did college papers, midterm exams, and complete semesters for inmates who just didn't want to do it themselves. I would earn a couple of books for a paper, and $175 worth of stamps for a complete semester's worth of work. I ran a store out of my locker selling ice cold sodas, chips, cookies, beans, and more, to inmates who either ran out of food mid-week, or didn't have money on their account to go to the store themselves but had their own hustle to earn stamps to buy food on the side.

It was a lesson in simple capitalism. I would buy a six-pack of soda for fifty cents per can and sell them for seventy five cents worth of stamps. Throughout the week, I would collect several books of stamps, keep some for my personal use, and sell the rest back to inmates. Those inmates would get the stamps immediately, and when it was our day to shop at the commissary later in the week, I would give a list of things to restock my store to each inmate that owed me. What started off as a couple of six packs of soda turned into a couple hundred dollars worth of stock each week. I would use my stamps to pay kitchen workers to steal whatever they could get their hands on—fresh produce, textured vegetable protein, tofu, vegan burgers—anything I could think of, they could somehow get their hands on it.

I used the stamps to fuel the local "economy" by paying people for their services. Everyone had a hustle, and if I could think of it, someone was more than willing to make it happen for the right price. I paid a guy that worked in the medical department to get me a forged slip saying I had foot problems so I didn't have to wear the required leather work boots to visits. I paid a guy in the plumbing department to steal a water filter off of the cop's water fountain and install it in my cell so I could have clean water. I paid my buddy to do my laundry once per week and iron my clothes when I had a visitor coming. I paid off the inmate in the intake department to convince the cop to make the top bunk in my cell appear occupied in the computer so I wouldn't ever have a cellmate.

Of course, I also used my stamps to write my friends and family. As a political prisoner, letters of support are your lifeline—they keep you alive and sane. To interact with someone on the outside is all you have to keep you connected. But without stamps, your letters are going nowhere. I wrote 1,500 letters while in prison, and I paid full price for about ten stamps when I first was locked up—otherwise I used the stamps I hustled.

Are the cooks prisoners or employees of the federal institution?

The entire kitchen and commissary is run by the inmates and overseen by guards. The guards facilitate the process, but the inmates do the cooking, cleaning, and prepping. They occasionally were involved in the ordering of the stock. While the menu was a fixed schedule, the ingredients weren't. For instance, every Wednesday they served burger and fries. Most of the times they made their own veggie burgers out of TVP and eggs. But occasionally, if it was cheaper to order veggie burgers by bulk, they would do so. Every once in a great while, they served vegan burgers.

I was good friends with the head cooks, so I had access to what brands they were using every week and the ingredients. However, I was more interested in what they could smuggle back to the unit for me to buy rather than eat it prepared in the chow hall. One Boca Burger Griller in the chow hall was nice, but a rack of twenty in my cooler hidden under my bunk was much better.

Do you get some food restrictions when under special conditions like isolation?

When you are in the SHU or on "lockdown" (meaning the entire prison is locked in their cells 24 hours a day for an unknown amount of time, ranging from days to months, for disciplinary reasons, like a riot) your food from the chow hall is brought to your cell, and you don't get any choice as to what is on your tray or in your bag. You also are cut off from commissary or given a limited shopping list for toiletries, but no food. That's why you keep a stash of extra food, just in case. I normally kept an extra jar or two of peanut butter, a box of granola, and some ramen soups under my bunk. The longest we were locked down for was seven weeks and it was a struggle, but I managed to maintain my vegan diet throughout.

Is there a medical health check regularly?

Medical checkups are available to inmates, but unless it's an emergency, like you've been stabbed, it's up to you to request one. For regular maintenance, like a dental checkup, I found that the general wait time was eighteen months before you are seen.

What is the reaction of the other prisoners to the fact that you are vegan? Do you get a lot of confusion?

Talking about veganism was a great way to interact with people that I normally wouldn't have and for people to understand my case and situation. Most people didn't really know what veganism was, and after learning about it they didn't understand why I just didn't eat animals while I was in prison.

After talking to them about my principles and why they didn't stop after entering prison, I gained a lot of respect from a lot of people. Folks in the kitchen started looking out for me, smugglers gave me first dibs on fruit and vegetables coming into the unit, and people were reading ingredients for me in the kitchen and commissary.

One of my favorite memories came almost two years in my unit after talking to people about veganism and why it was important to me. There was a riot on the yard, and we were on our second week of lock down and I was low on food supply. One day we were given an apple in our bag lunch. By the time the guard got to my cell on the top tier, she wheeled her cart full of bag lunches to my door and stopped. She gave a quick glance over her shoulder at the cameras mounted on the wall and opened the slot in my door. She handed me a bag lunch, and then started shoving apple after apple through the hole. After handing me about twelve apples, she told me people in the unit had refused theirs and asked that it was given to me instead so that I would have something vegan to eat.

Is there something you were really craving for, or do you just stop thinking of food until you know you'll actually be free and able to get whatever you want?

I craved good vegan food constantly. I had a subscription to a vegan magazine and I drooled over the food photos and ads constantly. But one of the things I actually liked about prison was the opportunity to be resourceful and see what you could get away with. Most of my time was not figuring out what and where my next meal was coming from, but how creative I could be with it. From faux chicken lo mien to deep fried apple pie pockets, the fun was in the adventure of it all.

ERIC MACDAVID

Eric MacDavid is currently serving a twenty years sentence in a federal prison, as part of the "green scare" tactics against environmental and animal activism. This is his testimony from jail as a vegan prisoner.
www.supporteric.org

I was arrested January 13, 2006 (both a Friday and a Full Moon). On the 17th I was brought before a magistrate and told that I was being charged with conspiracy to use explosives on government property and interstate commerce. After three weeks of trial in September of '07, in an attempt to utilize an entrapment defense, a kangaroo court came to its decision. Seven and a half months later, I was sentenced to 235 months in prison, given the "low end" of the sentencing guide-lines (because it was conspiracy the maximum was twenty years or 240 months). The reason given for the denial of a vegan diet during my time in county jail was that a vegan diet is a choice—not a religious or health issue. I was told that it could be set aside until I was no longer held there...and yes, after an amazing amount of support from folks on the outside and two hunger strikes, I was provided with meals that did not contain animal products. Not too long after I left, the menu was changed to all vegan meals. I encountered some health issues from that experience, like a heart condition called *paracarditus* where the protective tissue around the heart becomes inflamed and manifests itself in all sorts of chest pains, making laying down pretty much impossible. The federal prison system refuses to recognize vegan diets—it's all about labels and categories, though, only due to my heart condition, am I provided a "non-dairy, non-flesh diet". The commissary does carry some items which are absent of animal products, though they aren't there with that intent; and the bringing of food in from the outside was prohibited quite a few years ago—probably when they realized that they could make more money by cornering that market.

A vast majority of other prisoners commend me for sticking to my diet, and after inquiring as to why, they skirt the depth of the issues and their ramifications with jokes. I've not met other vegans in prison, though I know there are others, but I have run into a good number of vegetarians. The menu here runs on a five week rotation, with a daily 2,200 calorie diet. Breakfast begins a little after 6am and is open for around 40-45 min, lunch is anywhere from 10:45am to as late as 12:15pm, while dinner starts around 5pm and runs for about 45min.

At breakfast I have hot cereal, oat meal, grits, or cream of wheat and a piece of fruit; for lunch there is usually a soy alternative or beans, canned veggies, white rice or noodles or potatoes, and a piece of fruit; and dinner is a variation of lunch, minus the fruit. The only way to participate in the preparation of food is to work in food-service, otherwise it is off limits. Life in prison is basically a no-frills version of life out there (minus wimmin and those in between). Work is mandatory; there are places you can and can't go; there are cameras and cops, along with their bureaucratic handlers; there are the expectations of certificates/education/programming and they really do call it that. Visits are, by far, the biggest anomaly. Here it's four days per week (Fri-Mon), where from 8am to 3pm, those who are accepted onto my visiting list can come and sit in plastic chairs across from a little plastic table, share in over-priced vending machine items, a handful of which are vegan, and talk under the watchful eyes of cops and cameras. There's an embrace and kiss allowed at the beginning and the end. To get a hug during the picture, I have to buy a ticket through the commissary and other than that, contact is prohibited. That aspect has been the most difficult to dance with, seeing my partner and loved ones, and knowing that we much inhibit that one most basic impulse—to touch.

INDEX

agave (129, 137, 138)

alfalfa sprouts (40)

almonds (51, 53, 57, 129, 133, 137)

apple (96)

artichoke (96)

arugula (94)

asparagus (62)

banana (143)

barbeque sauce (81)

basil (43, 47, 51, 54, 57, 59, 65, 99, 101, 103, 105)

bay leaf (88, 104)

bell pepper (40, 43, 53, 71, 96, 101, 103, 112, 113, 124)

borlotti beans (37)

bread crumbs (75, 106)

broccoli (36, 61, 93, 103)

cabbage (114)

cannellini beans (88)

cardamon (111)

carrots (40, 55, 81, 85, 88, 93, 101, 105, 107, 113, 114, 124)

cauliflower (102)

cayenne pepper (124)

celery (81, 88, 105)
celery seeds (104)

chickpeas (65, 81)

chickpea flour (141)

chia seeds (124, 143)

chili (36, 47, 53, 59, 61, 66, 105, 108, 111, 154)

chives (142)

chocolate (133, 137)

cinnamon (111, 127)

cocoa (128)

coconut (103, 111, 133, 138, 154)

coffee (132, 138)

coriander (111)

cucumber (40, 112)

cumin (111)

curry (55, 93)

daikon (114)

dates (129, 143)

dijon mustard (81, 103, 142)

eggplant (38, 47, 65, 71, 96, 99)

flaxseeds (101, 124, 134, 143)

flour (59, 77, 86, 91,

93, 94, 96, 101, 106, 108, 118, 120, 122, 125, 128, 131, 134, 138, 162)

garbanzo beans (see chickpeas)

garlic (36, 43, 47, 51, 53, 54, 55, 57, 59, 61, 62, 65, 66, 71, 79, 81, 88, 94, 97, 99, 103, 104, 105, 106, 107, 108, 111, 112, 113, 122, 124, 125, 154)

ginger (114, 154)

gnocchi (91)

goji berries (143)

green beans (97)

green bell pepper
(see bell pepper)

hazelnuts (133)

hot sauce (49, 142)

kale (139)

lasagna (62, 65)

leek (101, 114)

lemon (38, 43, 103, 106,
124, 134, 142)

lemongrass (111)

lime (111, 154)

liquid smoke (81)

macadamia nuts
(128, 143)

margarine (75, 85, 91,
93, 94, 107, 122, 128, 131,
133, 134, 137, 138, 162)

marjoram (79)

meat substitute (66,
81, 104, 106, 107)

mint (40)

miso (114)

mushrooms (71, 79,
81, 94, 96, 97, 101, 107,
111, 114, 124)

mustard powder
(142)

nondairy cheese (47, 49, 59, 94)

nondairy milk (53, 54, 59, 62, 75, 85, 93, 111, 131, 132, 133, 134, 138, 139, 142, 154, 162)

nori (see seaweed)

nutmeg (59)

nutritional yeast (66, 75, 81, 82, 94, 102, 103, 106, 124, 139, 142)

oats (128)

onion (49, 65, 71, 77, 81, 82, 85, 93, 96, 97, 99, 104, 105, 107, 124, 141)

oranges (127, 143)

orange juice (128)

oregano (75, 96)

paprika (96, 103, 142)

parsley (53, 71, 94, 101, 103, 105, 106, 113, 124)

peanut butter (133, 154)

penne (47)

pecans (43)

pine nuts (103)

poppy seeds (134)

potatoes (61, 71, 75, 79, 82, 85, 91, 93, 97, 102, 103, 113)

pumpkin (71, 91, 114)

quinoa (79)

raisins (108, 131, 133)

raw (40, 43, 51, 112, 124, 129, 136)

red bell pepper (see bell pepper)

red onion (see onion)

rice (71)

rigatoni (53)

rosemary (37, 79, 88, 105)

rum (131)

sage (91, 104, 105, 106)

seaweed (114)

seitan (66, 104, 106, 107)

sesame seeds (86, 129)

shallots (111)

silverbeet leaves (40)

soy sauce (81, 104, 111, 114, 154)

spaghetti (49, 54, 66, 71)

spinach (59, 108, 112, 125)

sundried tomatoes (see tomatoes)

sunflower seeds (40)

sweet potato (114)
tahini (38)

taro root (102)

textured vegetable

protein (81)

thyme (79, 97, 101, 104, 106)

tofu (81, 103, 111, 114, 142)

tomatoes (43, 47, 51, 54, 57, 59, 65, 71, 99, 101, 112, 113, 124)

tomato paste/ passata (66, 81, 104, 106, 107)

vanilla (128, 131, 132, 138)

vegetable broth/ stock (61, 71, 85, 88,

96, 107, 113)

walnuts (59, 61, 81, 94)

wheat gluten (104, 106)

white onion (see onion)
wine (65, 66, 71, 97, 101)

zucchini (43, 49, 51, 55, 65, 71, 94, 101)

ACKNOWLEDGMENTS

My first thanks is to Giacomo—who opened my eyes and my heart five years ago and has always been with me since then.

Thanks to beautiful Kylie, Nat, and Susan.

Thanks to all the Sea Shepherd people and crew members that I have had the chance to cross the path, have tested my recipes on... sometimes with bad results, helping me to learn from my mistakes! Special thanks to all the Sam crew on Operation Zero Tolerance and Operation Relentless and to Iru, Eva, and Hillary.

Thanks to all the people I have worked with in the galley over the past four years, they have all inspired me and I owe each of them a little piece of idea here and there. Hope this book will inspire them too for further campaigns and time at sea...

A particular thanks to my friend Laura, chief cook of the Steve Irwin and author of the Sea Shepherd cookbook *Cooking Up A Storm.*

Thanks to Paul, for really making changes, and making people change. Thanks to my ever lasting friends Sibilla, Francesca, Marta, Sonia, Laure, Lucie, Cecile, after so many years and miles apart. Thanks to my Mum and to my Little Brother, that are my first food "fans." Thanks to Annie for creating a home on the other side of the world. Thanks to Gilles and Sylvie, Zac, and Kuma, an unexpected encounter in life. Thanks to Isa Chandra Moskowitz and Terry Hope Romero for the support